THE
NATIONAL
LOTTERY
BOOK

WINNING STRATEGIES

by
SAM WEREN

TAKE THAT LTD.

Take That Books is an imprint of
Take That Ltd.
P.O.Box 200
Harrogate
HG1 4XB

Adapted from Playing Lotteries for the Big Money

Australian Associate:
MaxiBooks, P.O.Box 529, Kiama, NSW 2533, Australia.

10 9 8 7 6 5 4 3

**You should take professional financial advice before acting
on material given in this book**.
The publisher, author, and their respective employees or agents,
shall not accept responsibility for injury, loss or damage
occasioned by any person acting or refraining from action as a
result of material in this book whether or not such injury, loss or
damage is in any way due to any negligent act or omission,
breach of duty or default on the part of the publisher, author, or
their respective employees or agents.

Given the potential rewards of winning the lottery, even a slight
advantage is worth grabbing. The National Lottery Book shows
you methods to help you choose numbers with which to play.
However, please remember *some* of these theories remain
unproven in the strictest scientific sense and may not increase your
chances at all.

ISBN 1-873668-70-8

Layout and typesetting by
Impact Design, P.O.Box 200, Harrogate, HG1 4XB.

Printed and bound in Great Britain.

Contents

1 WHY PLAY THE LOTTERY GAME?

Would you pay £1 for a chance to win £15 million? How about for the chance to win £10 million, to win £5 million, or even to win a 'meagre' £1 million? Well, experts estimate that upwards of 75% of British adults have a regular flutter on the new National Lottery in the hope of winning an enormous amount of money.

With rolled-over Jackpots of up to £15 million the National Lottery has captured everybody's imagination. Though the chance to win a fortune on the pools has been around for years, many people have dismissed them because they "don't know anything about football."

Premium Bonds also carry the chance of scooping £1 million, but these will probably always be perceived as an investment vehicle. The fact that each bond is carried-over into the next selection by 'ERNIE', only serves to lessen the excitement. There must be hundreds of thousands of people who have owned one Premium Bond since the day they were born and never checked the winning numbers.

The odds against winning the £1 million jackpot offered by the Premium Bonds is around 3.37 billion to one. Those against winning the lottery jackpot are 'only' around 14 million to one. However, the odds against winning any prize in the lottery is placed at approximately 54-1. That means anybody entering the lottery each week should register one win nearly every year.

COMING OUT AHEAD

Only the lottery offers you the chance to participate in each draw without any specialist knowledge. The chances of winning a big prize are supposedly equal for everyone. However, this report will show you how you can tip the odds ever so slightly in your favour.

You'll learn how the experts play... how the odds are calculated... why you can win bigger prizes... and you'll even be given some pointers on how to select numbers. On top of that, you'll learn the simple trick of 'trapping' and 'wheeling' numbers... techniques of money management... and a variety of other betting strategies.

Of course, sceptics will point out that the odds will still be against you. Read this report, follow the simple rules, use the systems of money management and bet wisely. Then, under the right circumstances, you may come out ahead in games of chance.

The companies who run lotteries may tell you their numbers are chosen entirely at 'random'. However, in reality, it is totally impossible to create a truly random process with physical materials. Every man-made device exhibits 'bias' over time.

ONLY IN AMERICA

The National Lottery may be new to Britain, but many countries have been running their own lotteries for years. Spain, Italy, Germany, France, Australia, Turkey, most South American countries and even China have their own versions of the National Lottery. In each of these countries one or two individuals strike it lucky and join the millionaire's club every month. But, without doubt, the absolute kings of the lotteries are the North Americans.

Most of the states in the USA now run their own lotteries. In 1980, only 13 different states had discovered the benefits that it can bring to their finances. This had ballooned to 28 by 1990, and today only a handful of old 'Bible Belt' states are resisting the march of the big-win lottery.

A peak of activity was reached in the New York State Lottery in December 1988, where 80% of the adults bought tickets to enter. At the start of the month the lottery had run with a 'usual' jackpot of a 'mere' $3 million. Nobody won that prize, so next week the jackpot rolled over to $17.5 million, and then rose to $26 million the following week. Despite the increased number of tickets sold as a result of the escalating publicity, still nobody won. These extra sales pushed the jackpot to a massive $45 million, and the state hit 'Lottomania'. More than 28,000 tickets were being sold over the counter each minute at over 5,000 lottery terminals around the state.

The draw finally took place in front of a record TV audience on Saturday night. By then, more than 37.3 million tickets had been sold. With so many people entering it was not surprising that there was more than one winner. In situations such as this the prize is split equally between the entrants with the winning numbers. Even so, you wouldn't have heard many of the 12 winners complaining about their bank balances increasing to the tune of $3¾ million!

Stable figures for Britain will take a time to be calculated, but the average spend per capita of New Yorkers on their lottery is around $92. That means each person spent approximately £60 during the year in the hope of winning the jackpot, which equates to around £1 per week. In terms of State Lotteries though, this is low. Massachusetts can boast an average spend of nearly £150 per capita.

WHOOPS

A lucky accident resulted in a $102,000 win for a Toronto woman. She went into her newsagent and asked for three tickets in successive lotteries. But due to a misunderstanding, the agent produced three tickets for the same lottery.

"He was most apologetic and offered to change them for what I really wanted," said the fortunate lady, "But I wasn't tempted to challenge fate, so I said I'd take the ones he had given me.

"The $100,000 winning ticket was the middle one. So if I'd only taken the one ticket I would have been one number from the first prize.

"I was one off the first prize about two years ago. I couldn't have stood it if it had happened again."

LARGE OAKS FROM
LITTLE ACORNS GROW

Lotteries can be traced back to ancient times. The first known public lotteries were run by the Romans during the reign of Augustus Caesar. Prizes in these lotteries are recorded as being money, slaves, and large villas (presumably the jackpot prize).

The bible even refers to a lottery with the prize being some of Christ's clothes. "Let us not rend it," says St. John in the book of revelations, "but let us cast lots for it."

Florence, Genoa and Venice all started lotteries around the 1530s to raise money for council funds. France followed suit with a lottery run by Francis I in 1540 to raise money for public works.

Prizes included money, slaves and large villas

Britain even copied these examples with Queen Elizabeth I running the first lottery in 1566 to finance the Virginia Colony (now the American state of Virginia).

That first lottery was such a success that a much bigger one was run in 1569 to pay for The Cinque Ports. Around 400,000 lots were sold at a cost of 10 shillings each and the prizes were tapestry, plate and money. A flutter on the lottery was only for the rich, since 10 shillings was a considerable amount of money in those days.

A number of lotteries followed. Perhaps the most notable being in 1627 and 1631 to pay for the delivery of fresh water to the city of London. Another in 1640 was run to help repair southern fishing fleets after the Spanish had knocked them about a bit.

The price of tickets continued to be set so that only the rich could afford to enter - a deliberate manoeuvre designed to stop poor people becoming poorer. But, where there's a will (or money to be won) there's a way. And in a lottery which provided over £70 million to help build Westminster Bridge in London and to establish the British Museum, it emerged speculators had bought the tickets and divided them into smaller, cheaper shares.

A huge number of dodgy dealings and side bets surrounded these first European lotteries, causing many to be outlawed, including the British National Lottery. It was in 1826 that a band of no-gooders ran off with the entire prize money never to be seen again. The Government was livid and the police completely lost for words. Who had perpetrated such a low down crime? Well, the answer is a group of Treasury Officials!!

Modern lotteries are believed to have started in the American state of New Hampshire in 1964. The more liberal attitudes of the 'swinging sixties' allowed some politicians to push through the required legislation. Far from being a trailblazer, this infant lottery was more like a damp squid. The organizers waited until a certain number of tickets had been sold until they made the draw. This meant you could wait weeks or even months for the winning number after buying your uniquely numbered ticket.

Like most things in America, a quicker result was required. The average American just wouldn't wait more than a couple of days to see if they had won. 'Hype' was needed.

New Jersey was the first to employ modern marketing techniques. They introduced a weekly draw and then followed very quickly with a daily drawing. Massachusetts went one better with 'instant' scratch-off cards, where you knew in seconds if you were a millionaire or not. However, it was the arrival of the computer's ability to sort large amounts of data very quickly which gave the industry a major boost.

Soon most states were offering lotteries where the players could pick their own numbers. Combining this player interactivity with multi-million dollar prizes meant lotteries soon became very big business.

As with the National Lottery, most states handed over some of the lottery proceeds to specific projects such as education, local arts, economic development and building new parks or play areas. Legislation was required to determine the exact split, and Britain has followed this example as well.

CONFIRMED BACHELOR

A Waverley truck driver who won £50,000 in the lottery says his bachelor status is by no means at risk, despite his good fortune.

"I've been a bachelor for 59 years and I've no intention of changing now," he said.

CHANGING SPOTS

According to statistics, lottery players are a fickle bunch. Sometimes projected sales can be wildly overstated and sometimes revenues are more than twice those expected. In other words, the people running the lottery don't know how much you are going to spend and when. This is reflected in various marketing exercises, not just in terms of publicity, but in the presentation of the lottery itself and the spread of prizes.

Essentially there are three main forms the lottery can take: the classic 'Lotto' game in which six numbers are picked in an attempt to win a possible jackpot; the simple Numbers Games of picking three or four numbers; and 'instant win' or scratch card games.

On top of those choices the frequency of the draw may be varied, the size and spread of the prizes can be altered, and the odds of winning can be 'tweaked'.

The odds of winning can be 'tweaked'.

In The States the marketeers have tried changing the name of the lottery, they've tried using themes, and they've applied many visual attractions on the card. In fact, anything to improve sales of tickets has been tried. California's lottery director once said you could sell cola as Classic Cola, Diet Cola, Sugar-Free Cola, Caffeine-Free Cola, New Improved Cola, etc., etc., but it is still essentially 'cola'.

Rest assured, your favourite lottery game, be it the new British National Lottery, or one of the continental European lotteries, the marketeers will soon be tampering with the format.

This report covers all the main forms of lottery and number picking. If your favourite lottery introduces an innovative approach, such as using letters instead of numbers, you can apply the same techniques as detailed in later chapters. For the mathematically minded, the number of combinations are likely to change with any change in rules. For example, using letters instead of numbers increases the number of permutations of any single selection on the card from 10 to 26. Please see chapter 5 for more details on calculating odds.

② DREAM WINNINGS

The huge sums offered in lotteries are the stuff dreams are made of. Who hasn't sat back and let go of reality, imagining how to spend the first million, let alone the rest.

Will you go on a round-the-world cruise? Will you buy an enormous mansion with acres of land? Will you snap up the latest Ferrari and a Porsche for your spouse? What about a yacht, the latest electrical goods, a large donation to charity or making your entire family comfortably well-off?

Perhaps your aspirations are more moderate - a week in the sun may be your idea of bliss. You may simply want to pay off your car loan, or buy a present for a loved one.

However big your dreams are, it is your dreams that the lotteries are really selling.

THE SIZE OF THE POT

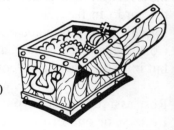

Would you prefer one chance to win £1,000,000 or 1,000 chances to win £1,000?

The top prize, or the size of the pot is the lottery marketeers ultimate weapon. Most people won't be turned on by a prize of £1,000, even though there aren't many who would turn the money down. There could be 1,000 prizes of £1,000 but the response of the public would not be all that much greater. But if you put it all together into one big prize of £1,000,000 heads will start turning and tickets will be sold.

Lottery marketing experts agree that they are not around to sell mathematical formulae to their customers, they are employed on a large human relations exercise. They know large prize pots attract entrants, but they also know that winners have to be seen to have won.

The structure of any lottery is designed so there are many winners on show at the ticket purchase points. This builds the notion that many people are winning the big prize. Of course, it doesn't occur to many that all these people can't be winning millions of pounds. The posters show a multi-million pound prize and lots of winners - it must be worth entering!

The Massachusetts lottery in America is widely recognised as one of the best run and most successful lotteries in the world. James Hosker, the lottery director, took sales from 50 million tickets to 600 million tickets in under ten years. One of the reasons is that the prize money given out was raised from 45% of the sales value to 60%. "People want to see winners," says Hosker, "so why not give the entrants 60% of their money back? If they like your game they'll play it, and in the long run the profits will be greater."

MAKING IT HAPPEN

The large jackpot prizes on offer don't just happen by sheer weight of sales. Of the 40%, say, of the sales that are retained, all the distributors have to be paid, the Government has to take its slice by way of lottery duty, and the 'worthy causes' need to receive their donations. This would hardly allow the next jackpot to grow by a noticeable amount.

No, the jackpots are made to happen. In any one lottery running, around 20 to 25% of numbers will not be picked by any entrant. The prize money from those numbers are allowed to roll-over into the next lottery. Since the marketeers know their game, most of this is piled into the jackpot to make the draw more attractive.

For example, if the jackpot is £2 million with other prizes of around another £2 million. Say 25% of prizes are unclaimed because the numbers have not been selected. An extra £½ million will be carried forward to the next draw making a jackpot of £2½ million. This may continue for several weeks.

If the lottery owners are really lucky, one of the numbers that remains unchosen will be the jackpot itself. So in addition to the £½ million rolled over from the lower prizes, they can add the £2 million main prize to the next jackpot - making a very attractive jackpot of £4½ million.

Many countries and states have ensured that this happens more frequently by changing the odds. Obviously, if there are more numbers to choose, there will be more that aren't chosen. By increasing the numbers chosen from 6 out of 48 to 6 out of 54, the odds can be more than doubled from around 12 million-to-one to nearly 26 million-to-one!!

WINNINGS AND ANNUITIES

Should you ever be in the position of going to pick up your cheque for winning the jackpot, you could be in for a big surprise. This is because your winnings may not be quite as big as you've seen advertised.

Imagine the headlines "Local Lady Wins £1 Million" splattered across the newspapers. You proudly step forward, with photographers snapping away, to receive your cheque. And then you've got it, a massive cheque for... for.... for £35,000 !?!? "But what's going on," you say, "I thought I won £1 million."

Many multi-million pound jackpot winners have been and will be dismayed to discover they have actually won an annuity worth £1 million and not £1 million itself. In the above example, a £1 million annuity will pay roughly £35,000 after taxes in 20 annual instalments. Now while this is not to be sniffed at, it isn't quite the same as getting a cheque for the big one straight away.

One winner in Florida thought she was going to walk into her bank with a cheque for $55 million, but found she was only going to get $2.7 million each year for 20 years. The state of Florida lottery company had simply bought an annuity that would yield $55 million over 20 years. The value of the annuity, if cashed in immediately, would only have been $26 million. Most people might find such circumstances disappointing, but would make do with a paltry $26 million. However, this Florida winner did her nut.

It all comes back down to the size of the jackpot generating sales. Some, but not all, lottery companies have found the annuity route a great way of making their jackpots look massive.

Say a company takes in £9 million of sales. They will have to give 45%, say, to the 'good causes', and set aside approx 15% for operating costs, leaving £3.6 million. Now if the company wanted to boost sales by saying they had a jackpot of £4 million, they would find they were £400,000 down. So, they buy an annuity for £4 million, the cost would be a mere £1 million. And, hey presto, a profit of £2.6 million drops into their pockets.

Of course, this is a simplified hypothetical case, and the lottery companies would point to extra running costs, secondary prizes and taxes. However, the practice of buying annuities can dramatically increase the apparent size of jackpots.

18-YEAR-OLD MILLIONAIRE

A young unemployed woman from Picton became a millionaire at 18 when she won a lottery jackpot of £1,300,000. She called into a Picton newsagency with her boyfriend to check the tickets, with no idea that one of them could be worth an absolute fortune.

"The agent said: 'You've won some money'," she said. "I said: 'That's nice, how much?'", she continued, "Then when he told me I just screamed!"

The jubilant winner has been unable to get a job since leaving school after failing to get into University to do the course she wanted.

"I'll get advice and invest some of the money. I'll buy some property and help my mum and dad," the teenager said, "But I'm determined money won't change me as a person, though it is a wonderful feeling to know I'm a millionaire."

HUMAN IMPULSES

All of the marketing, the mathematics and the financial dealings are aimed in one direction - taking advantage of human impulse.

Are we all turning into compulsive gamblers?

No matter how many times someone is told how small their chances of winning are, they will still 'have a go'. If the entrant doesn't win, they somehow find it possible to blame themselves. Luck plays by far the largest part in whether you are going to win or not.

Are the lottery companies turning us all into compulsive gamblers? Probably not. Many studies have been initiated around the world and their results have been mixed. The consensus is that lotteries are no more likely to turn us into gamblers than the odd flutter on the stockmarket.

There are two widely reported stories regarding gambling. The first is of an American couple who sold everything they owned and bought $15,000 worth of tickets over a three month period. They won their $15,000 back plus another $1,000.

Another is of an Englishman who sold his house, furniture and car. Then he quit his job and flew over to Las Vegas. There he placed his entire assets on 'red' at the roulette table. The ball went round and he won. Not pushing his luck any more, he quit the game, cashed in his chits and returned home a richer man.

In both of these cases, the people were taking a huge gamble with everything they owned. But, they could not be described as compulsive gamblers.

The regular purchase of a £1 ticket for the lottery isn't going to ruin your family. Compared to the two examples above, it would be described as verging on the ridiculously conservative. Rather than turn somebody into a compulsive gambler, a flutter on the lottery is likely to bring a little excitement into their lives. The mere choosing of numbers can give a certain pleasure in itself - and it is this choice with which the majority of this book is concerned.

③ MAKING YOUR OWN LUCK

LUCK, n. 1. (Chance as bestower of) good or bad fortune. Fortuitous events affecting one's interests, persons's apparent tendency to be (un)fortunate, supposed tendency of chance to bring a succession of (un)favourable events. 2. Success due to chance.

PROBABILITY AND LUCK

Over the years many prominent scientists have studied the subject of 'luck'. Even relativist Albert Einstein spent some time studying the 'science' of gambling.

All of them concluded there is no such thing as 'luck'.

Scientific explanation of luck comes under the heading of 'The Laws of Probability'. These laws attempt to explain the 'spread' of results in particular experiments.

Tossing a coin can be described as an experiment. If you throw a coin into the air, there are two possible outcomes - either it will land 'heads' side up or 'tails' side up. In other words, there is a 50% chance of heads and a 50% chance of tails. Extrapolating this closer to the linguistic meaning of 'percent', if you toss a coin 100 times, you should get 50 results of heads and 50 results of tails.

However, in reality, you are more likely to get 51 heads and 49 tails. It could be 52 and 48, or 53 and 47. As you deviate from the 50/50 result, the chances get less. In other words, you are more likely to get a 40/60 result than a 30/70 result.

An important fact to note here is that statistics are an historical view. We would expect, statistically five heads and five tales from 10 throws of the coin. If we toss the coin and get five heads with the first five throws, the chances of getting a head with the next toss is still 50%. Even if you get nine heads, there is still a 50% chance of getting a tenth result of heads.

In fact, the whole use of available statistics depends on whether you fall into the frequentist school of thought or the subjective school of thought. But more of that in chapter 5.

Let's take another example closer to the case of lotteries which often rely on balls being pulled out of a bag.

Say there are 20 balls in a bag. All of these balls are white except one which is red. The odds of picking the red ball from the bag are 1 in 20, or 19 to 1 against.

Now say 20 people have a go at picking the balls. One will certainly pick the red ball - with 20 balls and 20 people, someone has to get the red ball. Can you say that person is lucky and the other 19 are unlucky? No, it was purely chance at work. Before any ball had been selected, it was impossible to state categorically which person would choose the red ball.

If the same 20 people repeated the experiment, the chances are a different person would draw the red ball. Repeat the experiment enough times, meaning several thousand times, and each person should draw the red ball an equal number of times.

BLACK CAT

A black cat has long been seen as a sign of good luck. And now a couple from the west coast can prove it. On the way home from buying their £1 lottery ticket a black cat ran across the road in front of their car. And you've guessed it, the ticket proved to be a £750,000 winner!

Analysis of probability and selection requires a fair degree of mathematical and arithmetical expertise, not to mention a keenly logical mind and an ability to argue your corner! Many people use computer programmes to make predictions due to the complex behaviour of gaming statistics. For anyone who is interested, and the serious lottery player should know what odds they are up against, a deeper discussion of probabilities follows in chapter 5.

Of course, we all know some people who seem to be inherently 'lucky'. If they stepped forward to the bag, you would somehow just know they were going to pull out the red ball. Others testify to knowing when luck is on their side. These people may not be lucky all the time, but something inside them tells them what numbers to pick, which slot machine to play or which card to twist. In these circumstances science has yet to catch up with an explanation.

A DOG'S LIFE

Lucky, a cross-bred alsatian, brought a huge dose of good fortune to his owner. It was during an early morning walk that Lucky's owner stepped into his local newsagent and made the entry which would change his life. The result was a win of over £1,250,000.

"It will be great getting away from the rat race," said Lucky's owner, "And it will be great knowing we can afford to get away from it all and look after the kids."

What was lucky's share of the lottery winnings? A giant-sized T-bone steak!

GETTING AN EDGE

With the odds stacked against you and no known way of influencing luck, you could say that all forms of gambling are destined to be poor investments. However, even with the odds against you, there are betting systems and money management systems that will allow you to come out ahead, in the right circumstances.

The best way of getting an edge is to employ your own scientific or logical methods of reducing the odds. You need to be able to manipulate the variables in your favour. This is the best way to greatly increase your chances of winning. You could try cheating, but you are more likely to end up on a 'wanted' poster than a 'winners' poster.

The biggest clue to getting the greatest edge is 'understanding'. Knowing the rules can account for at least half of the battle. The other half is a mixture of probabilities and betting psychology. Understand these three areas and you will be well on the way to tipping the odds in your favour. Remember the three winning factors: RPP - rules, probabilities, psychology.

You can employ these factors in any form of gambling from football pools to poker, as well as in entering lotteries.

Lotteries come under the category 'Games of Chance'. Everybody who enters these forms of games are reduced to guessing what is going to happen - there is no way of calculating the outcome beforehand. An equal number of players, with an equal amount of money to spend will have the same chances of winning.

The odds against winning a particular draw could be, say, 80,000-1. If you buy one ticket, the odds are obviously 80,000-1. But if you buy two tickets with the same number, the odds remain at 80,000-1. You could buy 1,000 tickets, but if they all had the same number on, the odds stay at 80,000-1.

Naturally you could opt to buy tickets with different numbers. If you were to buy 10 such tickets your odds would reduce to 80,000-10. While these odds are better, they are not much better and they are 10 times more expensive to achieve. Unless you have the sort of money that Mr Mandel could afford to wager below, you could simply find yourself with bigger losses.

Assuming you don't have an inexhaustible source of cash, you will need to apply some of the techniques detailed in chapter 6 - Playing Like the Pros. Here you'll be shown how to 'wheel' number combinations or play the 'traps' - including how to pick the numbers to play.

THE AMAZING STORY OF STEVEN MANDEL

Steven Mandel is a computer genius and, just as importantly, an extremely rich man from Australia. In 1993 he hit the news not once, but three times around the world for winning lotteries.

Mandel's system was the simplest of all and totally legal. Enter with every possible combination!

Twice Mandel managed to pull his coup in Sydney. Then the Australian authorities decided they had had enough, and outlawed block purchasing. So, it was time for Mandel to search the world for 'the big one'.

After months of investigation, Mandel hit upon the state lottery in Virginia, USA. This fitted the bill perfectly. Although there were two drawings each week, the lotto game was played as 6/44 (pick six numbers from 44 possible - see chapter 4) making millions less combinations than many other states which went as high as 6/54. The prizes were good too, with many people from the state playing regularly. What is more, in Virginia, at the time, there was no law against block buying of lottery tickets.

"We had been running our lottery in nearly the same format for many years," said the state official in charge of lotteries, "the very idea that someone would want to spend $7 million buying tickets just seemed preposterous."

"The very idea that someone would want to spend $7 million buying tickets just seemed preposterous."

Mandel explained his system, "Theoretically anybody can buy all the combinations required to win the lottery. And any high school boy or girl could calculate those combinations."

But no school boy or girl could afford the $7 million entry fee and they certainly wouldn't be able to pull off such a feat of organisation.

"We used 20 to 30 computers, 12 laser printers and 16 personnel working full time to complete the task," continued Mandel.

With two drawings every week, the syndicate needed to act fast. In order to get every combination entered in 72 hours, they decided to print their own tickets. Each ticket was an exact replica of the official tickets for sale in supermarkets around the state. They then came to arrangements with the supermarkets that they would swap the official tickets for the syndicates tickets. This was legal.

"We thought they were nuts," said the manager of one supermarket chain, "I couldn't believe that anyone would want to corner the market in lottery tickets. But one thing we do is sell lottery tickets. So if someone comes to us and says they want to buy 700,000 lottery tickets, we sure aren't going to chase them away."

The syndicate needed couriers who could be trusted with large sums of money, who could work quickly and who were good with numbers. So they hired a dozen accountants.

"They told us we were going to buy lump sum blocks of lottery tickets. But it wasn't until we got down there that we could appreciate the scale of the operation. I couldn't believe it!" said one of the accountants used by the group.

With the planning complete and deals worked out with the supermarket chains, the syndicate were ready to sit back and wait until the time was right.

"One Thursday we received a call," continued the accountant, "if the jackpot wasn't won in the next drawing, we were to drive down to Richmond and start work."

The jackpot wasn't won and the group moved into top gear. The prize waiting to be won was $27 million.

Mr Mandel had hired Anatalya Alix, an ex-paratrooper, to organise this military style campaign. For two days the plan worked like a dream. Then, on the third day, disaster struck.

"Part of a chain decided they had taken enough and went down on us," explained Anatalya, "they wouldn't take any more tickets."

With only 90% of the possible combinations covered the group stood to lose out, big time. All their computer brilliance and military style planning was about to go down the pan.

"As with all these games of chance," continued Anatalya, "it came down to luck. Our number was drawn, or should I say one of our numbers was drawn. That night we had six guys looking through boxes of tickets to find the winner. When we found it, we were all six feet off the ground." Mandel was telephoned straight away and he let out a great sigh of relief. Nobody else had chosen the same numbers, so they were the only winners - of a hard earned $27 million!

The state official looked wistfully into the air. "It's a testimony to their computer and mathematical skills," he said, "but that doesn't mean I don't hope they never come back!"

Just for the record, Mandel's winning combination was 8, 11, 13, 15, 19 & 20. The Virginia lottery relies on small balls being blown around in the air to be captures by six tubes. The syndicate's numbers actually came out in the order 13, 19, 15, 8, 11 & 20.

GENERAL TIPS

Before playing, please remember the RPP factors - rules, probabilities, psychology. It can't be stressed enough how important understanding these three elements can be to your efforts.

① Learn all you can about lotteries, not just the National Lottery. Most people lose their money whilst not understanding the intricacies of the game.

② There are no certainties. Sure-fire systems don't exist. Some are better than others, but you can lose with each and every one of them. A win can not be guaranteed.

③ Don't bet more than you can afford to lose. Set a low limit such as 1% of your salary.

④ Greed destroys winnings. With the lottery or any other form of gambling, quit while you are ahead. Set a level of winnings with which you are happy, and quit when you have reached it. Winning streaks can end at any moment.

⑤ There is no 'law of averages' on individual plays. Statistics are an historical view of events. Benjamin Disraeli was the first to write "There are three kinds of lies: lies, damned lies and statistics."

⑥ Don't try any form of gambling when confused through tiredness, drink or upsetting circumstances. You will not be able to think clearly and logically.

⑦ Have fun. If the enjoyment has gone out of playing the lottery or any other form of gambling, give it a rest.

4 TYPES OF LOTTERY

If you look at the lotteries available around the world, you will find many different forms. You will discover instant games, numbers games, straight and boxed games and Lotto games.

Even within these categories, you will find differences. A Lotto game may ask that you choose 6 numbers from 49 possible, or they may ask you to choose 8 numbers from a possible 60. Some may ask you to choose letters instead of numbers, or they could ask you to choose colours.

This book will concentrate on the 'industry standard' form of lottery. Do not worry if your favourite lottery differs from the examples - the principles remain the same.

LOTTO

Lotto games are *pari-mutuel*. This means the prize values are dependent on the number of people playing.

You choose six numbers of your own from 1 to 49. If these six numbers match the six numbers randomly drawn by the lottery company, you win the first prize. There may be other players who have chosen the same numbers, so you may have to share the top prize. In the British National Lottery this first prize will be between £1 million and £15 million.

If your choices match only five, four or even three of those drawn, you still stand to win a second, third or fourth prize. A second prize will be worth several thousand pounds, and a third prize will be worth around £65. Fourth prizes will exist for three correct numbers, but you will only receive £10. A special bonus ball will be drawn after the main six numbers have been selected. This ball only applies to those lucky winners who already have five correct numbers. If their 'spare' number matches the bonus number, they will increase their winnings to around £100,000

The exact odds against winning depend on the total numbers from which your favourite lottery draws the five or six winning numbers. Appendix A gives the total number of combinations for the more popular Lottos.

The British National Lottery requires you to choose six numbers from a possible 49 (6/49). From Appendix A you will see the number of combinations of six numbers thus chosen from a possible 49, is 13,983,816, or roughly one chance in 14 million. You can use the same method to calculate the odds against winning any prize. In summary they are, approximately:-

	Prize	Odds
6 correct numbers	£1-15 million	13,983,816
5 correct + bonus	~£100,000	2,330,636
5 correct numbers	~£1,500	55,492
4 correct numbers	~£65	1,033
3 correct numbers	£10	57
Any of above	any	54

You select your numbers by striking out your numbers on the 'playslip'. Each game is called a 'board' and you can make up to five entries with one ticket.

After completing your playslip, you hand it to the operator who gives you a printed ticket with your numbers as proof of entry. You must check these tickets carefully to make sure the correct numbers have been typed in. Don't forget to keep your ticket in a safe place.

INSTANT WINS

These games have been available in Britain for years but the new National Lottery instant win game became available in the spring of 1995.

Simply buy a ticket and follow the instructions on the card. You will probably be asked to rub off some silver boxes to reveal hidden markings. If your markings match one of the winning sequences you stand to win a prize.

Being an instant game, you should receive your cash there and then. However, in the interests of security, larger prizes may only be claimed by posting your ticket back to the lottery company. Always remember to get proof of posting and use insured post.

The coupon will have another covered box marked "Void if Removed". This allows the company to check your ticket is real and not a forgery. Naturally, if you remove this box, you can't win a prize.

Even if you don't win an instant prize, you may still have the chance to win a prize from a free draw. Fill in your name and address and all losing entries will be put into a draw for a bigger prize or unclaimed prizes.

Instant win tickets are dubbed 'bearer instruments' by the legal profession. This means the person who has possession of the card or who has signed it, is the person who will receive the prize. So make sure you don't lose it!

LICK THAT

Odelia, the owner of Casa del Gelato, an ice cream and coffee shop in Manly Wharf continued to play her local instant-win scratchcard lottery even though times were hard. She was working seven days a week just to make ends meet. Then Odelia's luck changed for the better. She scooped over £50,000 in one game.

"Times are still difficult for small businesses, and we've just been hanging on in there," said Odelia, "Now with this lovely windfall I'll be able to pay off my debts and have a nice little backstop to keep me going until the good times come back."

'NUMBERS' GAMES

You'll probably have first heard of these games from American mobster movies as the 'numbers racket'. They are still more popular in America than anywhere else, but they are catching on quickly in Europe.

As well as 'The Numbers Games', you may see them advertised as 'Pick 3' or 'Pick 4'. They are very similar to Lotto but with smaller odds and smaller prizes. They may appear in the future in Britain.

Straight Games

You choose three or four numbers and if the digits match those which are drawn out of the hat, then you are a winner. Draws for this type of lottery are usually more frequent than for Lotto, often daily.

The numbers usually have to match those drawn in order as well as in digits. For example, if you choose 1234 you will only win if 1234 are drawn out of the hat. If 1243 are drawn out, you lose.

The odds against winning a straight Pick 3 game are 1:1000. The payout is usually around £500 for £1. For a Pick 4, the odds against are 1:10000.

Boxed Games

Boxed games give you better odds than straight games. In these games you must select two digits the same, for example 244. You win if your digits are selected in any order - 244, 424 or 442 for the above example. The odds against winning are reduced (by a factor of three for this game to 1:333), so expect correspondingly lower prize values.

The above example is a three-way box. A Pick 3 six-way box is where you must select three different numbers, for example 567. There are six ways of winning; 567, 576, 657, 675, 765 & 756. The odds against winning a six-way box are 1:167 and payouts are typically £80 for £1.

Some lotteries allow you to win if you pick the first two digits correctly irrespective of your third choice. This may be called a 'Front Pair'. It is the same as playing a rarely offered two-way box. The odds against winning are 1:100 (since there are 10 ways to win in a 1:1000 game) and payouts are around £50 for £1.

A 'Back Pair' is the same as for the front, but you must guess the second two digits correctly. The odds and winnings are exactly the same for a Front Pair.

A Pick 4 four-way box is run by picking any four digit number with three digits the same. A choice of 1555 would win if the numbers 1555, 5155,

5515 or 5551 are drawn. Four winning ways at odds of 1:1000 give odds against winning a four-way box at 1:2500.

You saw how a six-way box worked for Pick 3 and there is a similar game for Pick 4. Select any four digit number with two pairs of digits, for example 4488. You win with 4488, 8844, 4884, 8448, 4848, or 8484. Six ways of winning gives odds against of 1:1667.

Should you see a twelve-box game, you will need to select a four digit number with only two digits the same. There are, as the name suggests, 12 ways to win giving odds against of 1:833.

Finally, there is the twenty-four-way box. Select any four figures and if they are drawn in any order you are a winner. Odds against are 1:417.

The next chapter deals in more detail with how to calculate the odds against winning any particular lottery game.

5 MATHEMATICS OF PROBABILITIES

Good fortune or chance are totally subjective views. Many esoteric arguments can be raised as to the meaning of good fortune or the chances which surround everyday happenings.

Looking at the sky you could say, "There's a good chance it will rain today." You could sniff the air and say, "There's a chance we are having pizza for dinner." Both of these would be reasonable statements if the data (the colour of the sky or the smell) gathered by experimentation (looking at the sky or sniffing the air) indicate truth.

But at what point should you pack your umbrella or head for the dining table. There are many situations such as these when it would be helpful to know a bit more about the different levels of chance. For example, if there were only a 30% chance of rain, you may choose not to take your umbrella.

Obviously there is a need to replace ambiguous statements with something more substantial. The transition from intuition (black clouds mean rain) to science requires the introduction of probability.

Chapter 3 discussed the tossing of a coin and the probability of it landing 'head' side up or 'tails' side up.

If you throw one coin into the air, the outcome is completely uncertain - you don't know if it will be heads or tails. If you throw the same coin many times, the result becomes nearly certain - you will get nearly 50% heads and 50% tails.

But at what stage does this transition from uncertainty to near certainty take place.

Two schools of thought spring up around this very problem, and your view of statistics will be determined by which school you fall into.

The frequentist school, or objective school, asserts that the probability of getting a result of heads in a single experiment is given by the proportion of heads that would be found in a long series of experiments. As the data builds into, say, many thousand results, the effect of a single toss fades into insignificance.

This approach seems to be very attractive, appearing to be both practical and objective. But it does have problems. The first and main problem is that it isn't practical in 'real life' at all. A computer may be able to simulate tens of thousands of coin tosses or lottery drawings, but you can't carry out those many experiments.

Another problem with the frequentist approach is that not all problems can be covered by its approach. What is the probability of your hair spontaneously dropping out in the next ten minutes? You wouldn't have to consult your diary to know that your hair has never spontaneously fallen out in a ten minute period. So how can you use a large number of samples to make a probability prediction?

To put this in context; can we say a lottery will never draw the numbers 1,2,3,4,5,6 just because no lottery has ever done so? The simple answer is an emphatic - NO!

SCIENTIFIC PROOF

A syndicate of scientists from a hospital demanded documentary proof when they were told they had picked up £2,000,000 in the lottery. They were not disappointed. "When we saw it in black and white, we were elated," said one of the 15-strong syndicate. "No one believed it initially," said the doctor heading the team, "being scientists, we naturally wanted more proof."

The team took a short break at the local pub to celebrate their win, then it was back to work. The news of their record breaking win had come at their busiest time of the year.

The second school of thought is the subjective school. This school rejects frequentism by concluding there is no objective way of measuring probability. Therefore, they believe probability is really a degree of belief held by a person.

Some seek to qualify the basic belief. They say the probability depends on the degree of belief so long as the opinion is rational. Any opinion should be altered to encompass the facts as discovered by experiment, but should rely on belief anyway.

For example, you could believe the chances of getting heads with the toss of a coin is 1:5. However, tossing a coin 100 times would soon tell you that this is not the case. Your belief could then be rationalised to, say, a probability of 1:2.1.

This updating of beliefs is associated with the 'Bayesian' approach to probabilities. The Rev. T Bayes developed his theorem in the eighteenth century. However, it should be noted that the theorem is accepted by both Bayesian and classical statisticians. It is purely the interpretation and use of the result which causes the controversy. A full description of the theorem is beyond the scope of this report, so you are directed to one of the many excellent books on advanced statistics.

A question to ask yourself before deciding to which philosophy you will subscribe, is how many is 'many'. A lottery could only be drawn every month. That is a paultry 12 experiments a year. If you take ten years worth of data, does 120 satisfy the frequentist approach? Can computer simulations really replace the mechanism by which your lottery is drawn?

A few chances:-

Winning the top Premium Bond prize	3.4 billion - 1
Winning first prize in the lottery	14 million - 1
Throwing nine successive 6's with a dice	10 million - 1
Being involved in a road accident	200 - 1
Being dealt three of a kind at poker	46 - 1
Throwing any double at craps	5 - 1

PERMUTATIONS

Permutations concern the ordering of distinguishable items or events. Let's call these events $x_1, x_2, x_3, x_4, x_5, x_6, x_7$ and so on up to x_n where 'n' is any integer. These events 'x' can represent real objects or abstract ideas, but in lotteries they could represent the balls being drawn from the bag.

The x's are all distinguishable in that they are different numbers in the draw. This assumes, as in most lotteries, that when a ball is drawn from the bag, it is not replaced, and no other ball has the same number. Therefore, the x's are all well defined. So $x_1, x_2, x_3, x_4, x_5, x_6$, will be recognisable (distinguishable) from $x_3, x_4, x_2, x_1, x_5, x_6$.

Now let's say that the integer 'n' is 50 - the number of balls, or discreet numbers, which could have been pulled out of the hat. Provided there are no rules about how balls can be selected there are 50 possibilities for your first choice, which, once made, leaves 49 balls from which to make your second choice. When you have chosen your second ball, there remains 48 balls from which to make your third choice, and so on. Since any choice of ball is allowed at each stage, the number of different permutations:-

$$50 \times 49 \times 48 \times 47 \times 46 \times \ldots\ldots\ldots \times 5 \times 4 \times 3 \times 2 \times 1 = 3.041 \times 10^{64}$$

That's approximately 3 with sixty-four zeros after it.

But worry not! This is would only be your odds against winning if you had to choose all 50 numbers in the correct order.

A shorthand form of writing the above calculation is 50!.

It is not essential that you label all the balls as 'x'. You could have labelled some as 'y', so your sequence of six events could have been $x_3, x_4, x_2, y_1, y_5, y_6$. So long as all the x's represent different numbers, all the y's represent different numbers and all the x's are different numbers to the y's, the number of permutations is still 50! (pronounced fifty-factorial or factorial-fifty) for fifty possible numbers, 48! for forty-eight numbers, 44! for forty-four, etc.

If you only want to select six numbers, say, from the set of 50, the number of permutations is greatly reduced to:-

$$50 \times 49 \times 48 \times 47 \times 46 \times 45 = 11,441,304,000$$

This can be written as $50!/44!$, or in shorthand as $_{50}P_{44}$.

More generally it can be shown that

$$_{n}P_{r} = n!/(n-r)!$$

Where 'n' is the number of objects or balls, and 'r' is the number of samples.

HONEYMOON HAPPINESS

Bride-to-be Jacqui from Bowing very nearly forgot to put her lottery entry in because she was so busy with arrangements for the forthcoming wedding. But she's glad she did. As she pondered over holiday brochures with her fiancee Kevin, the news of her £150,000 win came through.

"It's unbelievable," exclaimed a doubly excited Jacqui. "We are not going to change the honeymoon, but I might upgrade the wedding cars," laughed Kevin. "And we've just bought our first home, so we can clear the mortgage almost straight away!" added Jacqui, "Then I'll give my mum back her cheque for the reception."

COMBINATIONS (SELECTIONS)

Now let's say that all the y's are the same, or not distinguishable from one another. So, x_3,x_4,x_2,y_1,y_5,y_6 is indistinguishable from x_3,x_4,x_2,y_5,y_1,y_6 as will be any 3! of the permutations obtained by rotating the y's amongst themselves while the x's stay where they are. In fact, we could now write any of the sequences as x_3,x_4,x_2,y,y,y since $y_1,y_5,y_6 = y_5,y_1,y_6$. That is to say, although the y's could be different numbers, they may occur in any order. Most lotteries allow the numbers to be in any order, even though they are often displayed only in ascending order.

Making the order of y's irrelevant decreases the number of possible permutations of the six events by 3!. The new number of 'permutations' becomes 6!/3! or $(6 \times 5 \times 4 \times 3 \times 2 \times 1)/(3 \times 2 \times 1) = 120$.

Now let's say the order of the x's is also unimportant. The number of 'permutations' must be divided by another 3!. So you now have:-
$6!/(3! \times 3!) = 20$.

Another way of thinking of this is that you have six possible positions which you can fill with three x's and then the remaining positions with three y's. That is to say, you could draw three balls from a bag and leave the other three inside. The order in which you picked the balls is not important, neither is the 'unchosen' order of the remaining balls.

The number of *combinations* of six taken three at a time is denoted by $_6C_3 = 6!/(3!3!)$.

If there had been four y's and three x's you could have written $_7C_3 = 7!/(3!4!)$.

If you had chosen the positions for the y's first, the number of combinations of seven taken four at a time would have been:-
$_7C_4 = 7!/(4!3!)$.

So, $_7C_4 = {_7C_3}$.

A generalisation of this rule indicates that the number of combinations of 'n' events taken 'r' at a time is:-

$_nC_r = n!/r!(n-r)!$

So the number of combinations of 49 taken 6 at a time (the total combinations of different groups of six in a 6 from 49 game) would be:-

$$_{49}C_{76} = 49!/6!(49-6)! = 13,983,816$$

So your chances of winning with one set of numbers in a 6/49 lottery would be roughly one chance in 14 million. In a different lottery, say 6/54, the total number of possible combinations of different groups of six is:-

$$_{54}C_6 = 54!/6!(54-6)! = 25,827,165$$

PROBABILITY

The use of probability in lotteries is an idealisation of the real situation. This is made because it could be helpful to know the chances of various outcomes. As the discussion at the start of this chapter shows, it is not a clear cut issue.

The estimation of 'chance' requires the substitution of something derived from logic. Frequentists and subjectivists will use different logic. In the majority of situations the two approaches agree with one another - but not in all. Lottery theory CAN fall into this category.

DOUBLE STRIKE

Who says lightening doesn't strike twice in the same place? Whoever they were they were wrong! A widow from Wollongong in Australia won $100,000 in her local Jackpot Lottery 4979. Pledging to share her luck with her invalid brother, the pensioner recounted a previous win by her late husband. "Back in 1972 he won the first prize of $60,000 in the lottery," she said.

"I've always been lucky," added the happy pensioner, "It all started when I was born on the 13th of the month."

Probability theory is an art which deals with statements such as:-

$$P(X)=0.8$$

meaning the probability of event X occurring is 0.8, 80%, or 8:10.

For the mathematician, event X is a symbol which can be manipulated according to rules fitting the physical realisation. The physical theory can only be determined operationally.

If you say P(X)=0 this means it is impossible for event X to occur. If you say P(X)=1, the occurrence of X is a certainty.

The event 'non-X' is simply a new event. It corresponds to the fact that event X does not occur.

Now assume there is a totally different event called 'Y', and a corresponding event 'non-Y'. We can introduce events 'X or Y' and 'X and Y'.

In the examples at the beginning of this chapter, X could be the event of it raining today, and Y could be the event of pizza for dinner.

The events X and Y could be independent or incompatible.

If they are independent, they are not related to one another in the slightest. In other words, the fact that it is raining has nothing to do with whether you'll have pizza for dinner or not. This could be determined operationally, by noting that supermarkets don't sell out of pizza ingredients when the forecast is for rain. But how do you cope with a household where the cook always makes pizza to cheer the family up when it is raining?

If the events are incompatible, they can't occur together. This would mean it can't rain if you have pizza for dinner and vice-versa.

Clearly, our example events are, usually, independent but not incompatible. This is the same for the probabilities of drawing numbers in a lottery. If you draw the number 14, say, it does not mean you can't draw any other number.

We can write:

i) $P(X) = 1-P(non-X)$
ii) $P(X or Y) = P(X) + P(Y)$ if X and Y are incompatible.
iii) $P(X and Y) = P(X) \times P(Y)$ if X and Y are independent.
iv)   P(Y, knowing X has happened) = P(Y) if X and Y are independent.

The assertions i, ii and iii are intuitively correct, satisfying the beliefs of the subjective thinker. If there is a 70% chance of it raining this afternoon, clearly there is a 30% chance of it not raining. If Y is incompatible with X, say, "it will hail this afternoon" (objections from meteorologists overruled!), and has a probability of 15%, it seems fair to say the probability of rain or hail is 85%. Similarly, in our independent example, and if the probability of pizza is 50%, it is reasonable to say the probability of pizza and rain is 70% x 50% = 35%.

Assertion (iv) is a little harder to argue. This means that the probability of having pizza for lunch is 50% even if we know whether it has rained that afternoon or not. The intuition of most people would say this assertion holds for the pizza/rain example and for the case of lotteries.

However, please consider the following.

Let Z be the initial state of the system to be considered. It could, for example be a lottery bag before any numbers have been drawn.

Now let one of the balls be drawn out of the bag. The situation has changed over time. Time being a vector in the forward direction, in our universe at least and as far as we are aware, we can define a Time Evolution Function F_t. The new state of the system is $F_t(Z)$.

Now, this is where it gets a bit complicated, let X be a set of points which describe the initial conditions of the bag with your first number having been drawn, which can not be distinguished. Anybody who has played the children's game of 'matchsticks' will know the future states are highly dependent on initial conditions. So, $F_t(X)$ can not be described as small. Removing one ball from the bag will certainly move at least one of the other balls and will probably make several move. So, $P(F_t(X)) \neq P(X)$

Let Y be a set of points which describe the conditions of the bag with your second number having been drawn. Part of the set Ft(X) will be in Y, part will be outside. The intersection ($\cap$) of points is described as: $F_t(X) \cap Y$

From assertion (iii) above regarding independent events:

$$P(F_t(X) \cap Y) = P(F_t(X)) \times P(Y) \neq P(X) \times P(Y)$$

In other words X and Y could be said to be not independent. And the results of a lottery are not purely random, but dependent on a set of initial conditions.

How can this be interpreted physically?

Say the 49 balls are stored in a box before the draw. They may be stored in numerical order, to ensure no balls are missing. Whoever puts the balls into the bag could always put the balls into the bag in the same order. Therefore the initial conditions could always be similar. Since the numbers drawn will vary even with the slightest difference in force of one ball being drawn out. However, anyone studying the numbers drawn from the bag may notice some numbers occurring more frequently than others.

"A bit far fetched!" you may argue. And you would have an argument, as does anybody where probabilities are concerned. But this theory is firmly believed by casino operators, who have a larger set of experiments to look at than anybody else. They specifically instruct their roulette croupiers to vary their wheel spinning motions. Any who are too consistent are quickly removed!

It may, therefore, be subjectively argued that the results of lotteries are not random until proven by experiment (lots of drawings).

COOL WINNERS

A 67 year old pensioner was struggling to live on around £65 a week until he became an INSTANT MILLIONAIRE with a First Division lottery win. As a father of four, from Chester Hill, he said he would share his win with his family and plans a future 'on easy street'.

"I've never contemplated how I would spend a million before," said the delighted pensioner, "I've only got a bottle of beer in the fridge, so I'll crack that open while I think about it!"

Perhaps he should team up with Helen of Harbord who won £12,000 from Camelot's instant win. She invested part of her win in a brand new state-of-the-art fridge to replace her 30 year-old trusty cooler. Now she has plenty of room for storing beer or even champagne.

PSYCHOLOGY & EQUITABILITY

So far we have only looked at the equitable facts of chance with regard to lotteries - those which can be related to the prospects of success.

You should also be aware of the inequitable factors which are around in pari-mutuel betting. Apart from the effects on relative wealth caused by taxation and deductions for running costs, you should note that it is essential you bet against the crowd in order to come out ahead.

Selecting or betting on numbers which are over-supported lead to abnormally low returns. This holds in betting on horse racing and football pools as well as for lotteries.

The lottery companies are well aware of inequitable effects. If they did not exist the companies would be ruined by what is known as The Law of Conservation of Wealth. This law indicates that capital is gradually attracted from the poor to the rich when risked on games of chance. While the company is richer than any one participant in the lottery, they are certainly poorer than the total wealth of everybody entering.

Several psychological trends have shown up in research which could help you increase the size of your winnings. The use of sequences is discussed in chapter 6 below. Another concerns spacial selection.

Spacial Selection

It is well known in the media that text for advertisements and books tends to 'drop' on the page when someone reads it. This obviously doesn't mean that the text physically moves, it is just a visual illusion. The human eye will see the space at the top of the page to be larger than the one at the bottom. To compensate for this, many advertisers allow a larger margin at the bottom of a page than at the top, to make the page seem more balanced.

When looking at a list of numbers available for selection, 1 to 48 or 1 to 54, the same illusion will occur to the entrant. Their selection area will be seen as a box with the earlier numbers appearing to have a larger area than those at the bottom.

Now, the entrant will usually want to spread his or her selections across the entire range of numbers available from 1 through to 48, for example. So, a greater than average number of selections will come from low numbers, eg: 1 to 30. In tests, asking entrants to select their numbers in an even spread across the range, there was a definite statistical skew towards the lower numbers which occur higher on a written list.

AGE OLD PROBLEM

A northern man watched in glee as five of his six lottery numbers dropped into place. Fingers, toes and everything else crossed, he pleaded with the TV screen for his sixth number to signal a jackpot win. His final number, 39, had been chosen because it was his wife's age.

Potential joy turned to anguish as the final number dropped - it was 38. "Why couldn't you have been a year younger," he cried to his wife. "But I am!" came the astonished reply.

The man told reporters that the agony of winning only £350 instead of £135,000 was nothing compared to the agony of getting his wife's age wrong.

Dates

An analysis of actual prizes won in American lotteries showed that when the majority of numbers in a drawing are in the range 1 to 12, the average prizes won were lower than for other drawings. When more than half of the numbers drawn were over 31, there were relatively few winners with higher prizes.

Why are 1-12 such bad numbers, and why do some experts recommend using numbers over 31?

Bear in mind how people will be selecting their numbers. There will be a high proportion of people selecting their birthday, or the birthday of a friend or loved-one. Think of your own birthday and then of everybody you know. Write them down if you have to. Do you notice anything?

Unless you are using some obscure form of calender, all the numbers you have written down will consist of a day and a month, and perhaps a year. The first number will be from 1 to 31, since the maximum number of days in a month is 31. The month number will be from 1 to 12. And finally the year will be 1900 and something.

Obviously all the numbers in the month range also appear in the day range. Just think how many times these will be selected by the population. Would you like to share your jackpot prize with fifteen people just because their second-cousin's granny has a birthday on 12th March?

The year range can be largely ignored with the exception of the number 19. Most people with disposable income, i.e. betting on the lottery, will be around 20 to 40 years old. The year suffix relating to their birthday will be around 55 to 65. These numbers are not available for selection in most lotteries.

You will also note at this stage other popular or unpopular numbers. What is your view of 'lucky' number 7, or 'unlucky-for-some' number 13?

Remember, your aim is to bet on numbers which other people will not.

⑥ PLAY LIKE THE PROFESSIONALS

A glance at Appendix A will show that the odds against winning the first prize in Lotto are, quite frankly, enormous. So why play in the first place. The main driving desire has to be the knowledge that someone will win and it will change their life forever - and that person could be you.

Given that you are going to have a 'punt' anyway, you might as well try to lower those astronomical odds in your favour.

THE WHEELING TECHNIQUE

People will tell you that there are no ways of improving the odds in a game of pure chance. They are wrong.

A technique reputedly developed by a European mathematician called Robert Serotic allows you to tip the odds in your favour. The technique is called 'wheeling'. It does not guarantee a win, far from it, but it does greatly increase your odds of winning, especially a second or third prize.

In extreme cases wheeling can lower the odds to 1:500 against. This may still seem high, but it is better than millions to one against.

It greatly increases your odds of winning.

A testimonial to Serotic's system is his own success rate. He is reported to have won nine lottery jackpots in 20 years with two in successive weeks.

It works by you picking any set of numbers. You could choose seven, eight, nine, ten or more favourite numbers. Obviously the more numbers you are playing with, the better the chances of 'your numbers' coming up.

You then select any five of your numbers and systematically 'spin' the combination of remaining numbers from your set. With each spin, you add one of the 'unused' numbers.

Let's take the example where you want to play 9 favourite numbers which you have chosen for one reason or another. And let's say the six winning numbers are going to be in your set.

The only way to guarantee that you win the jackpot is if you played each possible combination of those 9 numbers. This would normally cost you £84 to play. However, using a 5 from 6 wheeling system you could play only 18 games for £18 and still guarantee that one of your games would contain at least five of the six winning numbers - giving you a second prize worth several thousands of pounds.

So you see 'wheeling' is about improving your returns. In the above example, would you have rather risked £84 in order to win the jackpot. Or would you have rather risked £18 with the guarantee of winning at least a second prize?

LOST DEPRESSION

Two young mothers, both suffering from depression, can now live life a little easier. The first, a 38 year old mother of five, whose ages range from seven to 22 years old, won over £430,000. "I have been struggling to make ends meet for a long time, and I only decided to buy a lottery ticket on impulse!"

The second magic mum is an unemployed single mother who won more than £125,000. "I've been out of work for more than eight months and I was becoming rather depressed," she said, "This will relieve the pressure while I continue job hunting. But first of all, I'll get out of this rented flat and into a decent home."

WHEELING IN MORE DETAIL

Matrices are sets of numbers which can be written down, for the purpose of this book, in a generally rectangular shape. They consist of rows going across and columns going downwards.

The following is a 3x2 matrix:

$$
\begin{array}{ccc}
1 & 22 & 13 \\
8 & 9 & 14
\end{array}
$$

This is a 2x3 matrix:

$$
\begin{array}{cc}
1 & 22 \\
8 & 9 \\
12 & 24
\end{array}
$$

And the following is a 4x4 matrix:

$$
\begin{array}{cccc}
1 & 22 & 13 & 4 \\
8 & 9 & 14 & 12 \\
12 & 24 & 43 & 32 \\
9 & 25 & 38 & 39
\end{array}
$$

There are many rules for manipulating matrices, such as addition, multiplication and division. However, the only one which need concern us is substitution. For the 3x2 matrix, substitute these letters for numbers; 1=A, 8=H, 9=I, 13=M, 14=N, 22=V. You will get:

$$
\begin{array}{ccc}
A & V & M \\
H & I & N
\end{array}
$$

Simple, just swap the numbers for the letters.

Now let's get down to business. Imagine if you could play seven numbers instead of six. Your odds against winning would be reduced.

Write down the numbers one to seven. Then write the numbers you would like to play below these. For example, you may want to play 3,12,24,32,35,37,44. You will write down a 2x7 matrix:

1	2	3	4	5	6	7
3	12	24	32	35	37	44

Now, a Seven Number Wheel to play seven selections (games), would be a 7x7 matrix of the following form:

1	2	3	4	5	6
1	2	3	4	5	7
1	2	3	4	6	7
1	2	3	5	6	7
1	2	4	5	6	7
1	3	4	5	6	7
2	3	4	5	6	7

The numbers in the first row of the Seven Number Wheel were 1,2,3,4,5 & 6. Substitute your number 3 wherever the number 1 appears in the matrix. Then substitute your number 12 wherever you see the number 2 in the matrix. Continue to substitute your numbers from the 2x7 matrix into the 7x7 matrix to form the new 7x7 matrix for your own personal Seven Number Wheel (7 games) as follows:

3	12	24	32	35	37
3	12	24	32	35	44
3	12	24	32	36	44
3	12	24	35	36	44
3	12	32	35	36	44
3	24	32	35	36	44
12	24	32	35	36	44

Play one game for each of the rows in the matrix. That is to say, make seven entries for the above wheel, each with the numbers which appear on each row.

This Seven Number Wheel is a limited example. You may wish to play a lot more numbers than just seven. Say you have 12 numbers which you like, and which you think can make you rich. As before, write these down in a matrix. This time it will be a 2x12 matrix:

1	2	3	4	5	6	7	8	9	10	11	12
3	6	12	24	25	32	33	35	36	38	39	44

The exact number of games you would want to play will be determined by your own resources. ***Don't gamble more than you can afford to lose.*** Even using powerful techniques such as wheeling, the odds are against you winning. Set yourself a low limit, such as 1% of your salary and stick to it. The world is full of broken gamblers who thought, 'just one more go'.

Bearing the above in mind, say you want to play 18 games. The most effective Twelve Number Wheel (18 games) would look like the following:

1	2	4	5	7	10
1	2	4	7	8	10
1	2	4	7	10	11
1	3	4	6	9	12
1	3	6	7	9	12
1	3	6	9	10	12
1	4	5	7	8	10
1	4	5	7	10	12
1	4	7	8	10	12
2	3	5	6	8	11
2	3	5	8	9	11
2	3	5	8	11	12
2	5	6	8	9	11
2	5	6	9	11	12
2	5	8	9	11	12
3	4	6	7	9	12
3	4	6	9	10	12
3	6	7	9	10	12

Substituting your numbers as before, you will get:

3	6	24	25	33	38
3	6	24	33	35	38
3	6	24	33	38	11
3	12	24	32	36	44
3	12	32	33	36	44
3	12	32	36	38	44
3	24	25	33	35	38
3	24	25	33	38	44
3	24	33	35	38	44
6	12	25	32	35	11
6	12	25	35	36	11
6	12	25	35	11	44
6	25	32	35	36	11
6	25	32	36	11	44
6	25	35	36	11	44
12	24	32	33	36	44
12	24	32	36	38	44
12	32	33	36	38	44

Let's say the lottery was drawn and the numbers 3,25,33,35,36 & 38 were chosen. You would check your matrix and find you have won second prize with your game seven, and third prizes with your games one, two, eight and nine. That is one second prize and four third prizes. In addition, you followed our advice and chose more than half of your numbers over 31, which were drawn, so you would probably benefit from this draw by around £2,500 to £5,000. Not bad for a nominal £18 bet!

Obviously wheeling relies on 'spinning' numbers around your first selection and within subsets of your selection. Developing these wheels takes patience and a logical mind. That's why most people who want to get an upper hand use computer programmes to calculate their wheels.

Simple programmes which only calculate the wheels cost around £10 while the most sophisticated include autocorrelation trend analysis routines, highest winning system scans and redundant game deletion cost around £80. This may seem high, but the redundant game scan on its own can save you money every time you enter, and *it only takes a couple of third or fourth prize wins to recoup the cost many times over*. You'll find some recommendations on pages 123-125.

In the next few sections, the choice of numbers is discussed and the term Key Number is defined. If you choose to play Key Numbers, simply make the entire first column of your matrix equal to your Key Number. So the first number chosen will always be your Key Number. The same applies if you play two Key Numbers (or Key Number consisting of a pair). Always substitute in your Key Numbers first, then generate the Wheel in a similar manner to those two examples above, for the number of games you want to play.

Appendix B contains another couple of useful Wheels, to save you generating them for yourself.

KING OF KENO

$ "I hate to disappoint you," said the State Lottery Spokesman, "But that is not much for him. He would probably regard that as just right." *The Sydney Morning Herald* was reporting on a massive $7,500,000 win on Keno - a form of Lottery played in New South Wales, Australia.

The lucky winner was Zeijko Ranogajec who can not be described as an 'ordinary' lottery player. He is better known simply as Zeijko or 'The Joker' because of his fame as one of the best 'numbers' men in the world. He uses a computer programme more familiar to arbitrage dealers on the London Stock Exchange than to lottery players. As leader of a syndicate known as 'The Tasmanians', Zeijko travels the world playing lotteries, pools and betting on horses.

Those who have met him describe Zeijko as a quiet nervous man in his early 30's who puts in around 20 hours a day working out the numbers behind his betting strategies. Others say he is a well-dressed man with a card-players non-committal composure. Indeed, when he was told of his $7.5 million win, he simply left the club he was using as a base with barely a flush on his face. "He's big time, and I mean BIG time," said a fellow player.

In the late 70's Zeijko began subsidising his University education by playing blackjack at the casino tables. Before long he became well known in the casinos as a mathematical genius. At the time he was studying Commercial Law at the University of Tasmania, but his academic performance started to suffer as his blackjack abilities improved and he was placed on 'probation' by his tutors several times. When he finally left, he was also banned by the local casinos on the basis that he was a 'card counter'. Instead of letting that stop him, Zeijko simply went to a new location and started playing other games such as the pools and the lotteries.

Like all big betters, Zeijko relies on recouping 60-70% of his investment. In other words, for every £1 million he bets with, he will expect $600,000 back in minor prizes. He can improve that percentage slightly by coming to arrangements with the lottery terminal owners. These owners receive a cut of around 2% for processing lottery entries. Naturally, when someone like Zeijko turns up wanting to spend several million dollars, they are happy to give some of their profits back to the gambler.

That is how Zeijko came out ahead in the Sydney Keno game. He holed himself up in a private club with four lottery terminals and arranged for a constant procession of helpers to carry in boxes full of entry forms. Ironically, given his fame, the club would not give him any credit with which to play. So each day Zeijko turned up at the club carrying a cheque for $3 million.

Insiders say he spent around $29,000,000 in his six day search for the $7.5 million jackpot. He played 'quick pick' where his computer picked the numbers from his pre-programmed strategy, and placed 150 games on each ticket - the maximum - making each entry worth $150.

Apparently Zeijko was about $4 million to $5 million down by the end of the week when he finally cracked the jackpot. At no stage did he get flustered or anxious about the outcome. Instead he chatted with his ever-present girlfriend or spoke on his mobile telephone.

And the end result? A $2.5 to $3.5 million profit. Not bad for six days work!

PICKING YOUR NUMBERS

Wheeling allows you to pick as many numbers as you wish and arrange them so you have the best chance of winning any prize if your six numbers match those drawn out. The more numbers you pick, the better chance you have of winning. However, your required stake will also increase.

First you must select some numbers with which you want to play. A few instructions on how to select your numbers are given below. The logic behind many of these are given in chapter 5. However, you will no-doubt be keen to start playing, so if you would prefer not to wade through the section on mathematics, probabilities and betting psychology, just follow the instructions below.

- You may have as many numbers in your system as you wish, but more than six. A sensible amount would be eight to twelve numbers. It really doesn't matter how many numbers you have in your system, but try to stick to an even amount.

- Try to balance your number selection with odd and even numbers; with small and large numbers; with key numbers; and with number pairs.

- You should have an equal quantity of odd and even numbers. So an eight-number selection would contain four even numbers and four odd numbers. If you've chosen to play an odd amount of numbers, say 11, choose five odd and five even numbers before making your final selection.

- Make as many of your numbers as possible over 31 (not including 31). It would be a good idea to keep more than half of your numbers over this limit.

- Use numbers below 12 as sparingly as possible. These are not good numbers to choose if you want your winnings to be as high as possible.

KEY NUMBERS

The term 'key' is used in database management to describe a field which is common to two tables. And so it is with your lottery choices. Your Key Number will appear in each entry. It could be described as your favourite or 'lucky' number. You may also find a Key Number using the Hot System described in chapter 7.

Using one or more Key Numbers will substantially decrease the money you require to play a wheel.

Reduce the money you need to play a wheel

It is important that you use the above rules when picking your Key Number. That is to say, keep it above 12 and above 31 if possible. Of course, your own favourite number may not be above 31. However, a prize in the upper categories, first or second, will almost certainly be higher if you win.

The down side of using Key Numbers, is the plain fact that your Key Number must be drawn out. If it isn't, you can't win.

You may get an inkling of how powerful this technique is, by considering what everybody else is doing. They are playing one sequence of six numbers. For them, these are all Key Numbers. If those Key Numbers are not drawn, they will not win a prize. You on the other hand, have the luxury of only selecting one or two Key Numbers - which is easier than finding five or six.

If you wish to play two Key Numbers and reduce your required stake further, choose one odd and one even.

If you are short of cash or have four favourite numbers, choose two odd and two even. Whatever you do, try not to make these sequential such as 1,2,3,4 or 24,25,26,27.

A pair of numbers could be treated as one Key Number. This pair will always be played in any selection, as would a single Key Number. It effectively allows you to have three favourite numbers. In this case you would play your key pair and other Key Number as two Key Numbers. This method has one of the best records in lottery playing. The stakes are kept relatively low, and the results can be very productive.

SEQUENCES

Many other people will be playing sequences, so use sequences in your own selection with caution. (Please see Psychology and Equitability in chapter 5 above.)

The chances of the numbers 1,2,3,4,5,6 being drawn are just as likely as the numbers 9,14,21,26,31,43. It may seem impossible for six consecutive numbers to be drawn, but it is just as likely as any other six numbers in a truly random set. It has never been known for a Lotto game to draw six consecutive numbers.

Your best strategy is NOT to select consecutive numbers. There are so few sets of such sequences that many people will have selected them. Even if you won with six consecutive numbers, you would only end up with a small share of the winnings. Imagine winning £2,000,000 and having to share it with five thousand others. You'd only get £400!

Sequences don't have to be consecutive numbers. After all there are not those many possible selections of consecutive numbers. In a lottery of 6/49 there are only 44 possible six number consecutive runs. In a 6/54 game there are only 49 possible such sequences.

A sequence could be every fifth number, for example. It could be any number with a three and four in it (have you ever played fizz-buzz?). Or it could simply have a constant difference between the numbers.

As you can see there are many types of sequences, all of which are likely to have been chosen by the many millions of people who don't know to avoid such selections.

These are all sequences:

1	2	3	4	5	6	(consecutive)
10	11	12	13	14	15	(consecutive)
5	10	15	20	25	30	(every fifth number)
4	8	12	16	20	24	(every fourth number)
2	8	14	20	26	32	(add six)
3	11	19	27	35	43	(add eight)
1	2	3	5	8	13	(add the previous number)
1	2	4	8	16	32	(double previous number)
3	4	13	14	23	24	(Fizz-buzz revisited)
2	12	22	32	42	52	(all the two's)

And there are many more. Even if you don't consciously select a sequence, check to see if you have chosen one by accident.

Please do not make the mistake of taking this advice to its limits. That is to say, don't avoid any form of sequence in your selection.

Historical analysis of lotteries is useful in 'seeing' how numbers tend to come out. Of course, there is no scientific basis to suggest that these analyses can be applied to future lotteries, but not all scientific facts are known yet?

A pair of consecutive numbers, sometimes called 'twins', are drawn frequently. An example of twins may be the numbers 24 and 25. A massive two out of every three Lotto games draw twins. Also, in more than half of these, or more than one in every three Lottos, there is a third consecutive number. To continue with the example, this would mean the number 23 or 26 being drawn.

Four consecutive numbers, on the other hand, are highly unlikely to be drawn. Only one in a hundred Lottos draw such a sequence.

The trick is to bet on mini-sequences which nobody else will be betting on. Why not try some of the following? Each looks as if it is unlikely to come up, but they are just as likely as any other sequence and a lot fewer people will be picking them.

Example						Sequence
9	10	20	21	36	37	Three pairs
9	10	20	21	35	42	Two pairs, two singles
9	10	23	35	42	44	One pair, four singles
12	13	14	35	36	37	Two trios
12	13	14	23	35	42	One trio, three singles
12	13	14	23	24	42	One trio, one pair, one single
9	10	35	36	37	38	One pair, one quartet
5	22	35	36	37	38	Two singles, one quartet

These are examples only, and you should substitute your own numbers.

ON THE RAILS

A train driver played a simple 8 number wheel in the hope of winning the £750,000 jackpot. "My initial bet wouldn't have won," said the happy driver, "I was going to use the rest of my money to have a flutter on the horses, but decided to have another System 8 bet instead. And that's the one which won!"

"Now we can buy a house of our own - I was beginning to think that would never happen," he said.

BALANCED NUMBERS

Just as it has never been known for a lottery to draw six consecutive numbers, there are other trends that can be noted.

If your numbers add up to between 100 and 150, your chances of winning seem to be greater (in a 6/40, other limits apply for different lotteries as detailed below). If you are entering one of these lotteries, try to make sure YOUR six numbers add up to somewhere between 100 and 150.

Many hundreds of winners have followed this advice and won the big prize. In America Marie and Arthur Bonnan are reported to have won over $2 million with numbers which added up to 128. The next month a sole player, Steve Aarons, won $10 million with lottery numbers totalling 137. The winners aren't limited to America either. In Australia Ken Mathis won nearly $2 million in a lottery with numbers adding up to 143.

To find the sum of your lottery numbers, simply add the numbers, not the digits, together. For example:

$$4 + 12 + 18 + 23 + 32 + 39 = 128$$

and

$$1 + 5 + 25 + 28 + 36 + 40 = 135$$

Both of the above examples have a high total, between 100 and 150, and are balanced even to odd.

Other lotteries, as described earlier, require you choose six numbers from 44, 48 or sometimes 54 numbers. Here is a guide derived from historical data as to the total of your numbers:

6/36	Add up to 90-140
6/40	Add up to 100-150
6/44	Add up to 110-160
6/48	Add up to 130-180
6/52	Add up to 150-200

If your favourite lottery is one of those in the table, use the guidelines. If it is different, interpolate between the closest two examples in the table. For example the numbers in a 6/49 lottery should add up to around 135-185.

"It is a mathematical improbability that an unbalanced game with numbers that don't add up to over 100 will win a lottery. The big prizes go to players whose numbers total over the ton," says one mathematician.

REPEAT NUMBERS

It has already been noted that historical analysis does not necessarily help predict future drawings. However, there are many people who believe numbers certainly do repeat. In other words, some numbers seem to come up more frequently than would be expected in a purely random draw.

Since a large proportion of the people who believe in repeat numbers, appear to be computer 'boffins', it makes you think there could be something in it.

"I've been keeping a computer database of lotteries and pools for years," said one such computer expert, "and numbers certainly do repeat." Producing graphs of winning selections to back up his theory he added, "The large amount of data I've analysed can be subjected to a chi-squared test. Hypothesise that a certain number will be drawn and the test proves negative. Do the same for sequences and you'll get another negative result. But, hypothesise that any number will have a greater than average number of drawings, and you get a positive result." (Note: a chi-squared test is a method of testing whether or not a model is valid.)

The trick is to calculate how often a number has appeared in the past, and then use this data to predict when it will appear in the future and how often.

Another theory states that certain numbers are 'overdue'. This means that if a number hasn't been drawn out for a number of months, you should select it.

ANYTHING YOU CAN DO

A Campbeltown woman was shocked when her son and daughter-in-law won £50,000 on the lottery because she believed the odds of winning were so small. So imagine how she felt when she went one better only a few months later.

She had bought three tickets with successive numbers. It was the middle one which picked up the £50,000 prize, so the other two both picked up a £500 prize for being one away from the winning sequence.

"After enjoying such luck in the family already I didn't think it could possibly happen again - but I kept buying tickets just the same," explained the happy mother of four, "I'll probably take an overseas holiday, but beyond that I'm too confused to think clearly about what I'll do with my prize. It's nice to know I'll be financially secure in my old age."

7 NUMBER SYSTEMS

The next chapter will concentrate on helping you find inspiration for those lucky numbers - numbers which could make you rich. Some of these systems are accepted by lottery experts as conventional, others are not so orthodox. Each has been tried and tested in lotteries around the world. Read through them all, then choose which will suit you best. If none take your fancy, why not devise your own system.

DAY, MONTH AND YEAR

Your own birthday could hold the key to your winning numbers. This can provide you with any of the digits you need up to a maximum of eight (if you are playing wheels).

Perhaps you can follow the example of Augustin Jombo who won $26,000,000 in New York. His winning numbers were 6, 14, 15, 41, 45 & 51. He derived these numbers from his birthday - April 1951. First Augustin took the number of the month, then the digits of the year to give him 4, 1 & 5. Then he used these numbers with the reverse (reverse 51 to get 15), the sum (1 + 5 = 6) and combinations of the original numbers.

Should you feel your own birthday is not as lucky as you would like, why not use the birthday of a relative. Still not happy? Then try the birthday of a loved-one, a friend or of someone famous.

For example, Albert Einstein was born on 14th March 1879. Written numerically this is 14/3/1879. From this directly, you can extract the obvious four numbers 14, 3, 18 & 79. The latter number will need to be discarded because not many lotteries make you choose from 79 numbers (if it does, you should consider not bothering to enter!). Leaving you with the numbers 3, 14 and 18. You could use these as your first three selections and tag on three numbers chosen from another system. Alternatively, you could find another three numbers from someone else's birthday (your own?) to make up your six.

Other numbers can be derived from the same birthday. Writing the date without reference to day, month and year, we would write 1431879. This could yield the numbers 1, 43 & 18; or 14, 31 & 8; or 18, 7 & 9; or 1, 4, & 31.

Many exponents of the DMY (day, month, year) system believe you should simply take the last three digits of a famous birthday to form the first three numbers of your system. In Einstein's case, these would be 8, 7 & 9 or, written in order, a three number sequence of 7, 8 & 9. You already know that three number sequences appear quite often in lottery drawings, so Einstein's birthday would produce three good numbers from this system.

The day that you choose does not have to be a birthday. It could be the date of your wedding, when you first won a prize or when your friend last bought a round in the pub (what year was that exactly?). Another source of dates are important dates in history. For example Neil Armstrong and Buzz Aldrin became the first men to walk on the moon on 20th July 1969. This would

CLEAN SWEEP

Lucky cleaning lady Diane received a £10 lottery ticket from one of her clients as part of a Christmas box for her efforts during the year. Now she employs her own cleaning lady, after the numbers came up and made her a DOUBLE-MILLIONAIRE.

One of 13 children, Diane said she would be giving a bit to her brothers and sisters. "I don't own a home, so that will be high on the shopping list," laughed Diane. "Also, I've been planning a holiday to Perth and cutting corners on expenses for the trip. Now I'll be able to go First Class."

yield the number 2071969. Three numbers taken from this date could be 20, 7, & 19. Alternatively, you could choose 2, 7 & 19; or 7, 19, & 6; etc.

You may notice that a lot of numbers in these dates are 'wasted' because they are above 40, 48, 54 or whatever the limit is in your favourite lottery (49 in the British National Lottery). In this case, many people like to reverse the digits or to add the digits in order to produce a number which is within the required range. If the resultant number is one of your existing selections, a duplicate, add the numbers again.

As an example. Einstein's 'wasted' number was 79. Reversing this number becomes 97 - even worse! So add the digits of the number, $7 + 9 = 16$. This is within the range and could be used as one of your lucky numbers. If you have already selected the number 16, add again. This gives $1 + 6 = 7$.

If you are playing any of the Pick 3 or Pick 4 combination games, you will be looking for three digit or four digit numbers. The best ones to use for three digit numbers are the last three numbers of the year. The moon walking example would yield 969 which you would play in a Pick 3 boxed game. The Einstein example would yield 879.

Here are a few assorted famous birthdays of famous people to help you find your lucky numbers (all 20th century unless stated):-

JOHN QUINCY ADAMS	11/07/1767
JANE ADDAMS	06/09/1860
JOSEPH ADDISON	01/05/1672
WOODY ALLEN	01/12/1935
KINGSLEY AMIS	16/04/1922
MARIO ANDRETTI	29/02/1940
NEIL ARMSTRONG	05/08/1930
MALCOLM ARNOLD	21/10/1921
ARTHUR ASHE	10/07/1943
FRED ASTAIRE	10/05/1899
RICHARD ATTENBOROUGH	29/08/1923
DAVID ATTENBOROUGH	08/05/1926
WYSTAN HUGH AUDEN	21/02/1907
JOHANN SEBASTIAN BACH	21/03/1685

FRANCIS BACON	22/01/1561	MONTSERRAT CABALLE	12/04/33
JOHN BACON	24/11/1740	GEORGE CADBURY	19/09/1839
J.G. BALLARD	15/11/30	MICHEAL CAINE	14/03/33
ANNE BANCROFT	17/09/31	MARIA CALLAS	02/12/23
ROGER BANNISTER	23/03/29	GEORGE CAREY	13/11/35
HENRI BARBUSSE	17/05/1873	ANDREW CARNEGIE	25/11/1835
ROBERT BARCLAY	23/12/1648	WILLIE CARSON	16/11/42
RONNIE BARKER	25/09/29	FRANK CARSON	06/11/26
SUE BARKER	19/04/56	JACQUES CARTIER	31/12/1494
CHRISTIAN BARNARD	08/11/22	PABLO CASALS	29/12/1876
THOMAS BARNES	11/09/1785	FIDEL CASTRO	13/08/27
CECIL BEATON	14/01/04	BOBBY CHARLTON	11/10/37
KARL BEGAS	30/09/1794	NOAM CHOMSKY	07/12/22
JACK BENNY	14/02/1994	LINFORD CHRISTIE	02/04/60
CANDICE BERGEN	09/05/46	WINSTON CHURCHILL	30/11/1874
ERNEST BEVIN	09/03/1881	LUCIE CLAYTON	05/12/28
CILLA BLACK	27/05/43	STEPHEN CLEVELAND	18/03/1837
ROBERT BLAKE	15/08/1599	JAMES COBURN	31/08/28
CHAY BLYTH	14/05/40	CATHERINE COCKBURN	16/08/1679
ENID BLYTON	11/08/1897	CHRIS COCKERELL	04/06/10
DIRK BOGARDE	28/03/21	DENISE COFFEY	12/12/36
SIMON BOLIVAR	24/07/1783	NAT 'KING' COLE	17/03/19
BJORN BORG	06/06/56	PHIL COLLINS	30/01/51
LUCREZIA BORGIA	18/04/1480	WILLIAM COLLINS	08/09/1788
DAVID BOWIE	08/01/47	SEAN CONNERY	25/08/30
GEORGE BRADSHAW	29/07/1801	TOM CONTI	22/11/42
TYCHO BRAHE	14/12/1546	RY COODER	15/03/47
MARLON BRANDO	03/04/24	JAMES COOK	27/10/1728
LEONID BREZHNEV	19/12/06	ALISTAIR COOKE	20/11/08
BEAU BRIDGES	09/12/41	CATHERINE COOKSON	20/06/06
CHARLOTTE BRONTE	21/04/1816	IMOGEN COOPER	28/08/49
EMILY BRONTE	30/07/1818	C. COPERNICUS	19/02/1473
ISAMBARD BRUNEL	09/04/1806	JOHN COTTON	04/12/1585
YUL BRYNNER	12/07/15	COLIN COWDREY	24/12/32
WILLIAM BURKITT	25/07/1650	ANTHONY COX	18/07/15
RAYMOND BURR	21/05/17	QUENTIN CREWE	14/11/26
MATT BUSBY	26/05/09	DAVY CROCKETT	17/08/1786
MAX BYGRAVES	16/10/22	JOHN CROME	22/12/1768

OLIVER CROMWELL	25/04/1599
SYLVIA CROWE	15/09/01
PIERRE CURIE	15/05/1859
TONY CURTIS	03/06/25
R. D'OYLY CARTE	03/05/1844
LEONARDO DA VINCI	26/04/1452
ROGER DALTRY	01/03/44
CHARLES DARWIN	12/02/1809
STEVE DAVIS	22/08/57
LES DAWSON	02/01/33
HONORE DE BALZAC	20/05/1799
PIERRE DE COUBERTIN	01/01/1863
LEE DE FOREST	26/08/1873
CECIL B DE MILLE	12/08/1881
E. DE ROTHSCHILD	02/01/16
ALEXANDRE DECAMPS	03/03/1803
CHARLES DICKENS	07/02/1812
EMILY DICKENSON	10/1211830
DENIS DIDEROT	05/10/1713
JONATHAN DIMBLEBY	31/07/44
CHRISTIAN DIOR	21/01/05
FATS DOMINO	26/02/28
LONNIE DONEGAN	29/04/31
TERENCE DONOVAN	14/09/36
VAL DOONICAN	03/02/29
DIANA DORS	23/10/31
ARTHUR C. DOYLE	22/05/1859
MARGARET DRABBLE	05/06/39
RICHARD DUNWOODY	18/01/65
JO DURIE	27/07/60
GERALD DURRELL	07/01/25
BILLY ECKSTINE	08/07/15
STEFAN EDBERG	19/01/66
ANTHONY EDEN	12/06/1897
VIOLETTA ELVIN	03/11/25
DAVID ESSEX	23/07/47
KENNY EVERETT	25/12/44
CARL FABERGE	30/05/1946

G. FAHRENHEIT	24/05/1686
ADAM FAITH	23/06/40
FEDERICO FELLINI	20/01/20
FENELLA FIELDING	17/11/34
HARVEY FIRESTONE	20/12/1868
MICHAEL FISH	27/04/44
ROBERTA FLACK	10/02/38
ALEXANDER FLEMING	06/08/1881
JANE FONDA	21/12/37
HARRISON FORD	13/07/42
JOHN FOTHERGILL	08/03/1714
JOHN FOWLES	31/03/27
JOHN FRANCIS	03/09/1780
JOE FRAZIER	12/01/44
STEPHEN FRY	24/08/57
SANDY GALL	01/10/27
JAMES GALWAY	08/12/39
GRETA GARBO	18/09/05
GIUSEPPE GARIBALDI	04/07/1807
JUDY GARLAND	10/06/22
BAMBER GASCOIGNE	24/01/37
EUGENE GAUGIN	07/06/1848
IRA GERSHWIN	06/12/1896
JOHN PAUL GETTY	07/09/32

JOHN GIELGUD	14/04/04	THOMAS JEFFERSON	13/04/1743
KING CAMP GILLETTE	05/01/1855	ELTON JOHN	25/03/47
KITTY GODFREY	07/05/1896	HUGH JOHNSON	10/03/39
STEFFI GRAF	14/06/69	CARL GUSTAV JUNG	26/07/1875
ELISHA GRAY	02/08/1835	BORIS KARLOFF	23/11/1887
GERMAINE GREER	29/01/39	KENNETH KAUNDA	28/04/24
SIMON GUGGENHEIM	30/12/1867	JOHN KEATS	31/10/1795
JOSEPH GUILLOTIN	28/05/1738	HELEN KELLER	27/06/1880
LUKE HANSARD	05/07/1752	GENE KELLY	23/08/12
THOMAS HARDY	02/06/1840	NIKITA KHRUSCHEV	17/04/1894
JOHN HARVARD	29/11/1607	MARTIN LUTHER KING	15/01/29
GOLDIE HAWN	21/11/45	LAURENCE KIRWAN	13/05/07
WILLIAM HEARST	27/01/08	CALVIN KLEIN	19/11/42
EDWARD HEATH	09/07/16	CLEO LAINE	29/10/27
STEPHEN HENDRY	13/01/69	DINSDALE LANDEN	04/09/32
KATHARINE HEPBURN	09/11/09	BERNHARD LANGER	27/08/57
JAMES HERRIOT	03/10/16	NIKI LAUDA	22/02/49
FREDERICK HERSCHEL	07/03/1792	JOHN LE CARRE	19/10/31
MILTON HERSHEY	13/09/1857	LAURIE LEE	26/06/14
HEINRICH HERTZ	01/01/1894	PRUE LEITH	18/02/40
MYRA HESS	25/02/1890	DORIS LESSING	22/10/19
HERMANN HESSE	02/07/1877	JERRY LEE LEWIS	29/09/35
CHARLTON HESTON	04/10/24	PERCY LEWIS	18/11/1882
GRAHAM HILL	15/02/29	WILLIAM LILLY	30/04/1602
EDMUND HILLARY	20/07/19	CHARLES LINDBERGH	04/02/02
JAMES HILTON	09/09/00	ROBERT LINDLEY	04/03/1776
RICHARD HOE	12/09/1812	CAROLUS LINNAEUS	23/05/1707
JOHN EDGAR HOOVER	01/01/1895	LAURENCE LOWRY	01/11/1887
BOB HOPE	29/05/03	MARTIN LUTHER	10/11/1483
BOB HOSKINS	26/10/42	SANDY LYLE	09/02/58
JOHN HOWARD	02/09/1726	VERA LYNN	20/03/17
WILLIAM H. HUDSON	04/08/1841	DOUGLAS MACARTHUR	26/01/1880
DAVID HUGHES	16/05/1831	JAMES MADISON	05/03/1751
BASIL HULME	02/03/23	JOHN MAJOR	29/03/43
E. HUMPERDINCK	01/09/1954	EDOUARD MANET	23/01/1832
RAY ILLINGWORTH	08/06/32	BARRY MANILOW	17/06/46
HENRY JAMES	15/04/1843	NIGEL MANSELL	08/08/53
CLIVE JAMES	07/10/39	EDITH MARSH	23/04/1899

LOOK NO STICKS!

George Becket hobbled to the phone on his two walking sticks to answer a persistent caller. But the message nearly made him throw his sticks away and run round the room. He had won £50,000 in his local lottery. George, who had just left hospital after a painful hip replacement then called his life-long fishing buddy Dave Goldsmith with whom he had bought the winning ticket. Both spend a lot of time together and George said he planned to spend his half on a new 12-foot boat.

It was the second win for the lucky twosome. Just 12 months earlier they had shared £10,000.

KARL MARX	05/05/1818	RICHARD NIXON	09/01/13
GROUCHO MARX	02/10/1890	ALFRED NOYES	16/09/1880
PAUL MCCARTNEY	18/06/42	EDNA O'BRIEN	15/12/36
JOHN MCENROE	16/02/59	KATE O'MARA	10/08/39
MICHEAL MCINTYRE	29/06/56	RYAN O'NEAL	20/04/41
MICHEAL MEACHER	04/11/39	GEORG SIMON OHM	16/03/1787
MARGARET MEAD	16/12/01	AMELIA OPIE	12/11/1769
YEHUDI MENUHIN	22/04/16	GEORGE ORWELL	25/06/03
CLIFF MICHELMORE	11/12/19	ELISHA OTIS	03/08/1811
WILLIAM MICKLE	28/09/1735	IAN PAISLEY	06/04/26
ARTHUR MILLER	17/10/15	EMMELINE PANKHURST	14/07/1858
HUGH MILLER	10/10/1802	MUNGO PARK	10/09/1771
LIZA MINELLI	12/03/46	PETER PARKER	30/09/24
NANCY MITFORD	29/11/04	JAMES PARKINSON	11/04/1755
J. MONTGOLFIER	06/01/1745	LOUIS PASTEUR	27/12/1822
JOHN MOORES	25/01/1896	LINUS PAULING	28/02/01
MARILYN MONROE	01/06/26	JEREMY PAXMAN	11/05/50
IRIS MURDOCH	15/07/19	THOMAS PEACOCK	18/10/1785
ILIE NASTASE	19/07/46	GREGORY PECK	05/04/16
FLORENCE NIGHTINGALE	12/05/1820	SAMUEL PEPYS	23/02/1633
LEONARD NIMOY	26/03/31	FRED PERRY	18/05/09

MARY PETERS	06/07/39	RONNIE SCOTT	28/01/27
JEAN PIAGET	09/08/1896	GORDON SELFRIDGE	11/01/1864
JEAN PICARD	21/07/1620	OMAR SHARIF	10/04/32
PABLO PICASSO	25/10/1891	TOM SHARPE	30/03/28
LESTER PIGGOTT	05/11/35	B.WALLIS SIMPSON	19/06/1896
ISSAC PITMAN	04/01/1813	ANN SISSON	13/10/23
JENNY PITMAN	11/06/46	CYRIL SMITH	28/06/29
GENE PITNEY	17/02/41	MEL SMITH	03/12/52
SYDNEY POLLACK	01/07/34	MAGGIE SMITH	28/12/34
ROMAN POLANSKI	18/08/33	MURIEL SPARK	01/02/18
KARL POPPER	28/07/02	ELMER A. SPERRY	12/10/1860
ERIC PORTER	08/04/28	BENJAMIN SPOCK	02/05/03
NICOLAS POUSSIN	15/06/1594	WILLIAM SPOONER	22/07/1844
ENOCH POWELL	16/06/12	BRUCE SPRINGSTEEN	23/09/49
JOSEPH PRIESTLEY	13/03/1733	FREYA STARK	31/01/1893
ALAIN PROST	24/02/55	RINGO STARR	07/07/40
MARY QUANT	11/02/34	TOMMY STEELE	17/12/36
MARIE RAMBERT	20/02/1888	ROD STEWART	10/01/45
CHARLOTTE RAMPLING	05/02/46	BETTY STOVE	24/06/45
ALLAN RAMSAY	15/10/1686	ALAN SUGAR	24/03/47
OLIVER REED	13/01/38	HELEN SUZMAN	07/11/17
JIM REEVES	20/08/24	WALTER SWINBURN	07/08/61
CLIFF RICHARD	14/10/40	ERIC SYKES	11/03/1819
W. HEATH ROBINSON	31/05/1872	HENRY TATE	04/05/23
KENNY ROGERS	21/08/41	ELIZABETH TAYLOR	27/02/32
GINGER ROGERS	16/07/11	KIRI TE KANAWA	06/03/44
KEN ROSEWALL	02/11/34	EMMA TENNANT	20/10/37
PHILIP ROTH	19/03/33	BILL TIDY	09/10/33
FREDERICK ROYCE	27/03/1863	JOHN TOLKIEN	03/01/1892
KEN RUSSELL	03/07/27	DONALD TOVEY	17/07/1875
CHARLES SAATCHI	09/06/43	ANTHONY TROLLOPE	24/04/1815
YVES SAINT LAURENT	01/08/36	FRED TRUEMAN	06/02/31
VIDAL SASSOON	17/01/28	MAO TSE-TUNG	26/12/1893
JEAN PAUL SATRE	21/06/05	TINA TURNER	26/11/38
RICHARD SAVAGE	16/01/1697	MIKE TYSON	30/06/66
DOROTHY SAYERS	13/06/1893	JULES VERNE	08/02/1828
PRUNELLA SCALES	22/06/32	CHARLES VOSS	20/09/1815
CYRIL MEIR SCOTT	27/09/1879	EDWARD WADSWORTH	29/10/1889

BARNES WALLIS	26/09/1887
HORACE WALPOLE	24/09/1717
MUDDY WATERS	04/04/15
A. LLOYD WEBBER	22/03/48
FAY WELDON	22/09/31
G. ORSON WELLES	06/05/15
GEORGE WELLS	21/09/1866
SAMUEL WESLEY	14/08/1810
CHARLES WESLEY	18/12/1707
G. WESTINGHOUSE	06/10/1846
JUNE WHITFIELD	11/11/25
PAULA WILLCOX	13/17/49
FRIEDRICH WILHELM	02/01/1861
BOB WILSON	30/10/41
JOHN WISDEN	05/09/1826
ERNIE WISE	27/11/25
VICTORIA WOOD	19/05/53
PETER WOOD	08/10/28
WILL WORDSWORTH	07/04/1770
ORVILLE WRIGHT	19/08/1871
BILL WYMAN	24/10/41

SOUL PATH

R educing your birthday to a single one digit number is termed finding your Soul Path number. This is found by adding the day-number of your birth to the month-number, then adding the first two digits of the year, plus the second two digits of the year.

Thus 25th March 1976 would become 25/3/1976. This would be reduced using the Soul Path routine to 25 + 3, 1 + 9 and 7 + 6, giving 28, 10 & 13. Now add these numbers together to make one number, 28 + 10 + 13 = 51. To make a single digit number add the digits 5 + 1 = 6. So 6 would be the Soul Path number for anyone born on 25th March 1976.

The Soul Path number doesn't have to be played in a lottery on its own. You could play any set of numbers containing your soul path. For instance, you may choose to play 6, 16, 26, 36 or 46. You may go for multiples of 6 such as 12, 18, 24, 30, 36, 42 or 48. The number 36 is particularly powerful since it is the square of your Soul Path.

For those of you who have a Soul Path number of 1 to 4, say 3, you could also play numbers beginning with the Soul Path, for example 30, 31, 32, 33 (more powerful), 34, 35, etc.

WORDS AND NUMBERS

The 'Mystic Chart' is a well used alphanumeric system which enables anyone to use their name as lottery numbers. This, like the birthday system gives a very personal set of numbers.

This is the Mystic Chart:

1	2	3	4	5	6	7	8	9
A	B	C	D	E	F	G	H	I
J	K	L	M	N	O	P	Q	R
S	T	U	V	W	X	Y	Z	

Now take the first twelve letters of your name. Since we've analysed his birthday, lets use Albert Einstein again. The first twelve letters of his name are ALBERTEINSTE.

Consult the Mystic Chart and find the letter A. This lies directly below the number 1, so substitute 1 wherever the letter A appears in Albert's name. This is just at the beginning. Now find the letter L. You'll find it on the second row below the number 3. Substitute 3 for the letter L.

Continue this process of substitution and you will find ALBERTEINSTE translates into 132592595125. Now split this number into digital pairs. The sequence becomes 13, 25, 92, 59, 51, 25. Keep them in this order just for now.

The first two numbers 13 & 25 are satisfactory. However, the next three numbers, 92, 59 & 51 are all out of range for the average lottery. By now, you will have remembered that these numbers can either be reversed or the digits added together. Let's go for reversal in the first instance. These numbers become 29, 95 & 15. Only the second of these remains out of range. Add these numbers together to get 9 + 5 = 14.

The alphanumeric equivalent of Albert's name is 13, 25, 29, 14, 15 & 25. Have you spotted the duplicate? There are two number 25s. Reversal will yield a number out of range, so add 2 + 5 to get 7. Rearrange the numbers in ascending order and ALBERTEINSTE becomes 7, 13, 14, 15, 25 & 29.

Using your name to generate a set of numbers in this manner is called finding your Heart Number by many lottery writers.

One of the down sides of the Mystic Table when using names is the frequency with which vowels are translated. Vowels are the letters A, E, I, O & U. These emerge quite often in most names and words. You will notice that the letter E and hence the number 5 appears in ALBERTEINSTE three times. The numbers generated from your own name without the vowels is known as your Personality Number. Discarding these letters will mean that you probably need a middle name to get twelve letters.

NICE INITIALS

Elsie and Mick Heath from Maclean used the first eight pairs of letters in their children's names - Gary, Elsie and Mick - to generate their lucky lottery numbers. And that tried and tested method saw them finish £50,000 better off.

They had both been thinking that some new carpet for the house would be nice. However, the day-to-day demands on a family's finances kept pushing the carpet down the priority list. Now such an investment seems like 'small change' in the context of their big win.

THE BALANCED SUM SYSTEM

S tatistical analysis of previous lotteries can tell you a lot about the appearance of numbers, but would take a degree in statistics to work out for yourself.

The importance of this work was discussed in the section on balanced numbers. It was advised that your numbers should add up to somewhere between 100 and 150.

One method for calculating the exact sum for your numbers comes from the lottery itself. If you are playing a lottery in which you must choose your six numbers from 49, simply divide 49 by two and multiply by six. Half 49 is 24½, and six times 24½ is 149. So, as a rule of thumb, your numbers should add up to 149.

All the other games can be calculated in the same manner. A 6/44 equates to 128, which is calculated from 44/2 x 6 = 128. A 6/40 indicates your sum should be 120 and a 6/36 should be 108.

Lottery writers are quick to point out that lucky numbers chosen from birthdays and other anniversaries are unlikely to add up to the required number. In this case, you should 'throw in' a couple of high numbers to make the sum correct.

Say your numbers in a 6/44 lottery are 4, 12, 18, 23, 25 and 31. These add up to give:

$$4 + 12 + 18 + 23 + 25 + 31 = 113$$

Drop one of your lower numbers, say 4 since it breaks your rule of as many numbers as possible being above 12. The total drops to 109. This is 19 short of your desired total of 128. So, simply replace the number 4 in your selection with 19. Your new numbers will be:

$$12 + 18 + 19 + 23 + 25 + 31 = 128$$

THE HOT SYSTEM

The Hot System is a method of finding a Key Number to play the Wheeling technique or to use as your 'favourite' number. It is a derivative of the Alphanumeric System and makes use of the same Mystic Chart.

Simply take the first two letters of your names, including any middle names. Translate these letters into numbers using the chart. Then add each pair of digits to give one number. Repeat this addition with each pair of digits until you produce a one or two digit number within the range of your lottery or game.

Hot Numbers could help you zoom in on the jackpot

Using Albert again as an example. The first two letters of his first and second names are AL & EI. The numbers associated with these pairs of letters are 13 & 59. The first round of addition yields $1 + 3 = 4$ and $5 + 9 = 14$. Add the results to get $4 + 14 = 18$. So, Albert Einstein's Hot number would be the number 18.

Another example is Neil Armstrong. Space enthusiasts will know Neil's middle name is Alden. The moonwalker's letter pairs are NE, AL and AR. Consulting the Mystic Table you will find these equate to 55, 13 & 19. All three of these numbers could be within range of some lotteries and could be used with three numbers taken from, say, Neil's birthday.

Continuing with the Hot System, add $5 + 5 = 10$, $1 + 3 = 4$, and $1 + 9 = 10$. You have 10, 4, 10. You could play these numbers in a boxed game of Pick 3, and maybe take home a decent prize. Adding again gives $10 + 4 + 10 = 24$. This is within range and is Neil Alden Armstrong's Hot Number.

Your Hot Numbers could help you zoom in on the multi-million pound jackpot prize in the National Lottery.

EASTER SURPRISE

The dates for the religious festival of Easter are calculated from the position of the moon. Many people believe this to be of great significance and certainly not random. The date on which Easter falls in the year of your birth is used by many as a Key Number.

Others, in addition to their birth year, fill more of their selections by using the Easter date from the year they were married in, or the year in which their spouse was born.

Use the table below to find the date on which Easter fell in years which were or will be significant for you. Firstly find the row relating to the decade in the first column. So, for the year 1962, go to the row starting 1960. Then move across the table until you are under the last digit of the year, for 1962 this is the column headed '2'. Easter in 1962 fell on the date of the 22nd. If you were born in 1962, your Easter Number would be the number 22.

The dates of Easter from 1900 to 2029 are:

	0	1	2	3	4	5	6	7	8	9
1900	15	7	30	12	3	23	15	31	19	11
1910	27	16	7	23	12	4	23	8	31	20
1920	4	27	16	1	20	12	4	17	8	31
1930	20	5	27	16	1	21	12	28	17	9
1940	24	13	5	25	9	1	21	6	78	17
1950	9	25	13	5	18	10	1	21	6	29
1960	17	2	22	14	29	18	10	26	14	6
1970	29	11	2	22	14	30	19	10	26	15
1980	6	19	11	3	22	7	30	19	3	26
1990	15	31	19	11	3	16	7	30	12	4
2000	23	15	31	20	11	27	16	8	23	12
2010	4	24	8	31	20	5	27	16	1	21
2020	12	4	17	9	31	20	5	28	16	1

PLEASE LORD

The winner of £100,00 now has the opportunity to have his unconventional prayers answered. The 77-year old pensioner has been a keen lottery player for many years. Whenever he went to enter his numbers he carried with him a prayer written down by a friend. It read: "Please Lord, let me prove to you that winning the lottery will not spoil me."

The jubilant winner is totally confident he can stick to the terms of his prayer as proof of satisfaction for his Maker.

BIBLICAL NUMBERS

Throughout the bible there are references to numbers which repeat with alarming regularity. These numbers were intended to be guidance for the hazards found in everyday life. "As the scriptures give us a way to lead our life, the numbers in the New and Old Testaments act like roadsigns," says one religious writer. More used to translating ancient hebrew manuscripts than entering lotteries, he goes on, "Everything in the bible has at least two levels of meaning. Usually there is the initial story element, then there is a moral, and finally guidance on how to lead a better life. It is the same with the numbers which are mentioned."

Take for example the wilderness days of 40 days and 40 nights. Why was the number 40 so important?

Other numbers which arise from biblical writings can be extracted.

1 - There is only one God, Father and Holy Spirit. God only had one son.

3 - Three Wise men came to visit Christ when he was born and there is the Holy Trinity. There were also three crosses on Calgary Hill.

7 - On the seventh day He did rest. There were also seven years of famine and seven years of plenty (this could be a reference to 7 + 7 = 14 or 7 x 7 = 49 as well).

12 - The number of Apostles and the tribes of Israel.

13 - The number of letters attributed to Paul.

27 - The number of books in the New testament.

31 - The number of trees in the Garden of Eden.

40 - As in 40 days and 40 nights.

PRAYERS ANSWERED

A Hindu family of five living in a cramped flat in Canterbury literally had their prayers answered when they topped £50,000 in the lottery. Their syndicate's name was "Shiva K P Shakkti" which the winner explained was the God of Energy to whom he had been praying for relief from his family's domestic situation.

"I didn't ask for the world," said the father and family breadwinner, "Just a bit to help us put a deposit on a decent house. Now we can look forward to living a little more decently."

THE NUMBERS AVAILABLE

Many numbers have peculiar and fascinating facts about them which could cause some people to choose them for their lottery entry. You could opt to avoid them on this basis or use them for your own selection. :-

1   Kronecker, the 19th century mathematician, said the number 1 was the only real number. "God made it," he said, "All the rest are the work of mankind.". The first 'lucky number'.

2	Division into 2 parts is the most common in practice than any other division.
3	The second Lucky Number after 1.
4	The first composite number.
7	There are 7 days in the week. The third lucky number. Considered by many to be the luckiest number of all.
8	An octave is made up of 8 notes.
9	The fourth lucky number.
10	Our most common counting system is based on 10.
12	The year is divided into 12 months.
13	Accepted by many to be the unluckiest number of them all.
14	There are 14 pounds in a stone.
15	A snooker triangle contains 15 balls.
16	The most perfect, Perfect Number.
18	The age of 'coming of age'.
20	A biblical 'score'.
21	The total number of dots on a dice.
23	If you choose 23 people at random, the odds will be that two of them will share the same birthday.
24	There are 24 hours in a day. Also 4 factorial.
25	The square and sum of two squares as used in geometry $5^2=4^2+3^2$. Also the 8th Lucky Number.
27	The total points of the coloured balls on a snooker table.
28	The number of days in a lunar month.
30	The number of days in four of the 12 months.
31	The number of days in seven of the 12 months
33	The 10th Lucky Number.
34	Add up to seven, the luckiest number of all.
37	The 11th Lucky Number.
40	Life begins at 40.
42	The answer to Life, the Universe and Everything.
43	The 12th Lucky Number.
49	Seven squared, considered by many to be luck-squared. Also the 13th Lucky Number. The highest number available in the lottery.

LOCATION, LOCATION AND LOCATION.

A sk an Estate Agent which are the three most important factors to consider when buying a house, and you will get the reply "Location, location and location." You may also get the same answer from a lottery expert.

Several top American lottery writers believe you should derive at least four of your lucky lotto numbers from longitude and latitude coordinates. Most of them suggest a good combination is to mix these numbers with

Derive four of your numbers by this method

birthday numbers. Others prefer to take four numbers from the direct longitudes and latitudes and then derive two others by reversing or adding digits for numbers over 40 or 48.

For example, if you were born in Manchester with the coordinates 53o30N 2o15W. This means Manchester is 53 degrees 30 minutes north of the equator and 2 degrees 15 minutes west of Greenwich Meridian. It can be written as 53.30N 2.15W.

Since the first number is greater than 49, you should reverse it to produce the number 35. Alternatively, you could add the digits $5 + 3 = 8$. The second number is 30, the third is 2 and the fourth is 15. So your first four numbers become 2, 15, 30 and 35; or 2, 8, 15 and 30.

You may stick with these numbers and use two numbers derived from your birthday or you could return to the coordinates. Now add all the numbers in the latitude and the numbers in the longitude. You will get $5 + 3 + 3 + 0 = 11$ and $2 + 1 + 5 = 8$. Your winning combination, as indicated by the location of Manchester on the globe is 2, 8, 11, 15, 30 & 35!

Maybe you are playing any of the Pick 3 or Pick 4 games. In this case your numbers would be 533 or 215.

As another example. Perhaps your dream holiday would be in Rio de Janeiro, Brazil. The coordinates of Rio are 22.53S 43.17W. This gives you four numbers, 22, 53, 43 and 17. Obviously the number 53 is out of range so either reverse the numbers or add the digits. In this case we'll reverse the digits. So your first four numbers obtained from the Rio longitude and latitude are 17, 22, 35 & 43. Your two remaining numbers are derived from adding the longitude digits and then the latitude digits. You will find 2 + 2 + 5 + 3 = 12 and 4 + 3 + 1 + 7 = 15. Making your final winning selection 12, 15, 17, 22, 35 & 43. Rio here you come!

In the unusual case of you playing a lottery game with more than six numbers to select, experts suggest you add the 'degree' part of the coordinates to the corresponding 'minute'. For Rio the seventh number would be taken from 22.53S. In other words 22 + 53 = 75. Remember, when the number is out of range, reverse the digits or add them. Reversing the digits in this case is of no use, since 57 is also out of range. So adding 7 + 5 = 13 gives you your seventh number.

Similarly your eighth number, if required, will be 43 + 17 = 60; then 6 + 0 = 6.

Here are a few more locations to help you find your winning position.

ABERDEEN	57.10N	2.04W
ABU DHABI	24.28N	54.25E
ACAPULCO	16.51N	99.56W
ADELAIDE	34.56S	138.36E
AGUAS CALIENTES	21.51N	102.18W
AIME	45.33N	6.40E
ALICE SPRINGS	24.42S	133.52E
AMSTERDAM	52.21N	4.54E
ANKARA	39.55N	32.50E
BANGKOK	18.14N	99.24E
BEIJING	39.55N	116.26E
BELFAST	54.35N	5.55W
BELGRADE	44.50N	20.30E
BIRMINGHAM	52.30N	1.50W
BRADFORD	53.48N	1.45W
BRIGHTON	50.50N	0.10W
BRISTOL	51.27N	2.35W
BUENOS AIRES	34.40S	58.30W

CAMBRIDGE	52.12N	0.07E
CAPE TOWN	33.56S	18.28E
CARACAS	10.35N	66.56W
CARDIFF	51.30N	3.13W
CARLISLE	54.54N	2.55W
CORK	51.54N	8.28W
COVENTRY	52.25N	1.30W
DAKAR	14.38N	17.27W
DELHI	28.40N	77.14E
DENVER	39.45N	105.0W
DERBY	52.55N	1.30W
DUBLIN	53.20N	6.15W
EDINBURGH	55.57N	3.13W
EDMONTON	53.34N	113.25W
EXETER	50.43N	3.31W
GLASGOW	55.53N	4.15W
HARROGATE	54.00N	1.33W
HEREFORD	52.04N	2.43W
INVERNESS	57.27N	4.15W
IPSWICH	52.04N	1.10E
JAKARTA	6.08S	106.45E
JOHN O GROATS	58.49N	3.02W
KABUL	34.31N	69.12E
LANDS END	50.03N	5.44W
LEICESTER	52.38N	1.05W
LEEDS	53.50N	1.35W
LIMA	12.06S	77.03W
LISBON	38.44N	9.08W
LIVERPOOL	53.25N	2.55W
LONDON	51.30N	0.10W
MEXICO	19.25N	99.10W
MIAMI	25.45N	80.15W
MIDDLESBROUGH	54.35N	1.14W
MOSCOW	55.45N	37.42E
NEWCASTLE	54.59N	1.35W
NEW YORK	40.43N	74.00W
NORTHAMPTON	52.14N	0.54W
NORWICH	52.38N	1.18E

NOTTINGHAM	52.58N	1.10W
OXFORD	51.46N	1.15W
PERTH	31.58S	115.49E
PORT GENTIL	0.40S	8.50E
PORTSMOUTH	50.48N	1.05W
ROME	41.53N	12.30E
SAN FRANCISCO	37.45N	122.27W
SHEFFIELD	53.23N	1.30W
SOUTHAMPTON	50.55N	1.25W
SWANSEA	51.38N	3.57W
SYDNEY	33.55S	151.10E
TEHRAN	35.40N	51.26E
TOKYO	35.40N	139.45E
WASHINGTON	38.55N	77.00W

HALF AND HALF

A good neighbour bought her friend a lottery ticket as a 'going away' present. It was one of two, the other she kept for herself. The present was posted with a 'good wishes' card to the new address of her long time friend. Before it could reach it's destination the ticket had appreciated in value by more than 5,000,000%.

The ecstatic winner said she would send a letter back with a cheque for half of the winnings. "It was a gift," said the purchaser, "But if my friend is kind enough to want to share the prize with me, I'll accept graciously."

IT'S IN THE STARS

Many people look to the stars for guidance on daily matters via horoscopes. These involve the positions of particular stars relative to others. You may believe horoscope experts are able to make predictions of events from the positions of these stars.

Lottery numbers also can be found in the stars. Each and every star has a magnitude. This is a measure of how bright the star is. A high magnitude indicates a bright star, and a low magnitude indicates a dull star as seen from Earth.

The distance to the star can be measured in units called light years. Light years are used because the distances involved are so huge. Even the closest star is many millions of millions of miles away from the Sun. One light year is the distance light can travel in one year, at 299,792,458 metres each second! The Sun, of course, is the closest star to earth. Next closest is Proxima Centauri at 4.24 light years.

FORTUNE TELLER

Bill's wife, Zelda, was the only member of the household who was not surprised when Bill learnt he had become a MILLIONAIRE by winning top prize in the lottery. As a fortune teller, Zelda had foretold her husband's good fortune almost to the day.

Having worked as a milkman, a dry cleaner, and building worker and a refuse collector, Bill said he planned to work on for at least a little while longer as a supervisor for a transport company.

"I'm going to replace my old golf clubs with a brand new set," said Bill, "As for Zelda, she asked if we could spare £100... I think we'll be able to manage that!"

Take 'The Dog Star', Sirius, as an example. It has the official name Alpha Canis Majoris and can boast a magnitude of -1.47 at a distance of 8.7 light years from the Sun.

Extract for yourself the three digit number which can be used in Pick 3. It is the magnitude of the star written without the sign, in other words 147. These three digits can be added to give you one of the numbers required for lotto. For Sirius this first number is 1 + 4 + 7 = 12. The second number is taken from the distance of 8.7 light years. Adding 8 + 7 gives the answer 15. So the two numbers in the dog star are 12 & 15.

Why not check out the magnitudes and distances to the stars in your star sign. Some stars in ascending magnitude:

Acrux	1.39	370	Altair	0.75	16
Canops	-.71	98	Aldebaran	0.78	68
Arcturus	-.06	36	Spica	0.91	220
Vega	0.03	26	Antares	0.92	520
Capella	0.05	43	Fomalhaut	1.15	23
Rigel	0.14	815	Pollux	1.16	35
Procyon	0.34	11	Deneb	1.26	1600
Betelgeuse	0.41	520	Mimosa	1.28	490
Achernar	0.49	118	Regulus	1.33	85
Hadar	0.61	490			

SPORTING NUMBERS

Sports related numbers are all around you. Even if you are not an avid sports enthusiast, you will realise your daily newspaper is filled with the stuff. Clues to lucky numbers can be taken from your own sporting life or from these pages.

How did your favourite rugby team get on this weekend? Say they won 24-4, this could provide you with the numbers 24, & 4, or 2 & 44. You could also add all the digits to give you the number 10.

Other high scoring sports include basketball, cricket and snooker. Look for clues in all of these sports. Cricket is particularly good. You can generate numbers from team scores, individual scores, batting averages, bowling figures and extras. Then you have the second innings to look at!

Luck may already have played a part in the number selection process. Where did the jackpot draws fall on this week's pools coupon. Maybe fate is trying to tell you something. If you don't want to follow the crowd, why not select the game numbers which have produced the last six no-score draws.

Take a look at the horse racing pages. Apart from winning numbers of the horses, there are the race start times and the distances to derive numbers from.

THE CIRCLE SYSTEM

This is a spacial system. Rather than letting your conscience pick the numbers for your winning ticket, why not let your sub-conscience do the choosing. As with dreams, which are covered later, you may find there is more to your inner thoughts than you know.

Copy out the following table on a piece of paper. Make sure to keep the spacing about the same as is given here:

1	1	1	1	1	2	2	2	2	2
3	3	3	3	3	4	4	4	4	4
5	5	5	5	5	6	6	6	6	6
7	7	7	7	7	8	8	8	8	8
9	9	9	9	9	0	0	0	0	0
1	1	1	1	1	2	2	2	2	2
3	3	3	3	3	4	4	4	4	4
5	5	5	5	5	6	6	6	6	6
7	7	7	7	7	8	8	8	8	8
9	9	9	9	9	0	0	0	0	0

Now take a pen and draw a circle anywhere in the square of numbers, making it quite large. Make a note of the numbers which the circle passes through in an anti-clockwise direction. Repeat the exercise, but draw a pentagon - a shape with five equal sides. Again, make a note of the numbers through which the line passes. Finally, draw a triangle and make a note of the numbers.

All of the numbers you have written down will be single digit numbers since only the numbers one to nine have been used. So, make the numbers into pairs. For example the sequence 3, 7, 9, 1, 3, 5,... becomes 37, 91, 35,...

As before reverse any numbers out of range or add the digits. This should give you six to seven lucky Circular Numbers with which to play the lotteries. If you have more than six numbers, you can play a wheel system, or you can reduce the numbers by adding digits of each number and making new number pairs.

MUTUAL APPRECIATION

A pensioner from Calla Bay received five lucky lottery tickets from his son when he spent some of his spare time cleaning his son's car. One of them came up trumps and the father pocketed £200,000. "I'll split it three ways," he laughed, "One-third to my wife, one-third to my son and one-third for myself."

Bet the lucky winner's son is glad he had a dirty car!

A MATTER OF CHEMISTRY

The universe mainly consists of ordered elements. Anything that you can touch or see is made up of one or more of these elements. You may remember from school, that the arrangement of these elements is called the Periodic Table of Elements. But have you wondered why the elements exist in a particular order? The answer, of course, is unknown. Could this table hold the secrets to a lottery fortune?

There are two ways of using the table to find Key Numbers for use as a favourite number or in a wheel. Firstly, you could search out an element with which you find some synergy. This could be as fickle as liking the name or for any other reason. You then simply look up the Atomic Number of that element and use it in your lottery entries. (Remember, if the number is out of range, reverse or add the digits.) You may, for example, have an affinity to gold. The symbol for gold is Au, and you can see that it has an atomic number of 79. Add these digits, since they can't be reversed, to give 7 + 9 = 16. This would be a good number to use as a Key Number in the lottery.

Secondly, you can use it as an alphanumeric system similar to the Mystic Table. This Periodic Table system gives you far more permutations than the Mystic Table. The first 100 elements in the Periodic Table are listed below.

For example, Albert Einstein begins with the letter A, which is always a number 1 in the Mystic Table. But if you look down the Periodic Table, you find there is an element which begins with the let-

You may, for example, have a liking for Gold

ters Al. This element is aluminium and has an atomic number of 13. Therefore the first number associated with Albert is 13. The next two letters are B & E. Again, consulting the table, you will find an element called Beryllium which has the symbol Be and has an atomic number 4. The final letter pair is R & T. You will see there is no element with the symbol Rt, so you must find the closest alphabetically. This is Ru for ruthenium which has an atomic weight of 44. So, the Periodic Numbers associated with the name Albert are 13, 4 and 44.

Looking at the surname Einstein in the same manner:
The letters EI are closest to Er = 68. Add these digits to make 14.
The letters NS are closest to Np = 93. Reverse these digits to make 39.
The letters TE are given by Te = 52. Reverse the digits to make 25.
The letters IN are given by In = 49.

Albert Einstein would therefore generate seven Periodic Lottery Numbers from his name, they would be 4, 13, 14, 25, 39, 34 & 49. The best single entry with these numbers would be to drop the number 4. This would give an entry with half the numbers over 31 and none below 12 as highlighted in chapter 5.

Symbol	Element	Atomic No.			
			H	hydrogen	1
			He	helium	2
Ac	actinium	89	Hf	hafnium	72
Ag	silver	47	Hg	mercury	80
Al	aluminium	13	Ho	holmium	67
Am	americium	95	I	iodine	53
Ar	argon	18	In	indium	49
As	arsenic	33	Ir	iridium	77
At	astatine	85	K	potassium	19
Au	gold	79	Kr	krypton	36
B	boron	5	La	lanthanum	57
Ba	barium	56	Li	lithium	3
Be	beryllium	4	Lr	lutetium	71
Bi	bismuth	83	Mg	magnesium	12
Bk	berkelium	97	Mn	manganese	25
Br	bromine	33	Mo	molybdenum	42
C	carbon	6	N	nitrogen	7
Ca	calcium	20	Na	sodium	11
Cd	cadmium	48	Nb	niobium	41
Ce	cerium	58	Nd	neodymium	60
Cf	californium	98	Ne	neon	10
Ci	chlorine	17	Ni	nickel	28
Cm	curium	96	Np	neptunium	93
Co	cobalt	27	0	oxygen	8
Cr	chromium	24	Os	osmium	76
Cs	caesium	55	P	phosphorus	15
Cu	copper	29	Pa	protactinium	91
Dy	dysprosium	66	Pb	lead	82
Er	erbium	68	Pd	palladium	46
Es	einsteinium	99	Pm	promethium	61
Eu	europium	63	Po	polonium	84
F	fluorine	9	Pr	praseodymium	59
Fe	iron	26	Pt	platinum	78
Fm	fermium	100	Pu	plutonium	94
Fr	francium	87	Ra	radium	88
Ga	gallium	31	Rb	rubidium	37
Gd	gadolinium	64	Re	rhenium	75
Ge	germanium	32	Rh	rhodium	45

Rn	radon	96	Te	tellurium	52
Ru	ruthenium	44	Th	thorium	90
S	sulphur	16	Ti	titanium	22
Sb	antimony	51	Tl	thallium	81
Sc	scandium	21	Tm	thulium	69
Se	selenium	34	U	uranium	92
si	silicon	14	V	vanadium	23
Sm	samarium	62	W	tungsten	74
Sn	tin	50	Xe	xenon	54
Sr	strontium	38	Y	Yttrium	39
Ta	tantalum	73	Yb	ytterbium	70
Th	terbium	65	Zn	zinc	30
Tc	technetium	43	Zr	zirconium	40

LIGHTS OF YOUNG ABERDEEN

A young couple from Aberdeen are well on their way to buying their first home thanks to a £50,000 win in the lottery. "We've been renting and thought a home of our own was a long way off," said the wife who was expecting their second child in a few weeks, "My husband only recently got a job after being unemployed for 12 months, so times have been quite hard."

SENSITIVITY

Now is the time to start sensitising yourself to numbers around you in everyday life. A number throwing itself into your consciousness, no matter how, may be trying to tell you something.

● Do you notice numbers in conversations? If someone says they missed the 3 o'clock from Paddington and someone else says they have picked up three books from the library, make a note of the repeated number three.

- Take notice of numbers that 'jump' out at you from newspapers. If a football player with the number nine on his shirt catches your eye, write it down.

- Keep a note of numbers which appear on tickets given to you, or receipts you collect. The three figure number on your grocery bill could be a good choice for Pick 3.

- Don't ignore numbers related to irritation. If a train conductor gives you hassle, take a note of his number, not to complain, but to enter in the lottery. If a car cuts you up at the roundabout, note down its number.

- How many times a day do you look at your watch or the office clock? Maybe you looked at the time at 3:15. Maybe you looked at it again at 4:15. Instead of counting the hours to home time, make a note of the recurring number 15.

8 NUMBERS AND DREAMS

Sleep is an important part of all our lives. We spend nearly one third of our lives asleep. Without it we would certainly go crazy, since sleep is restorative and human growth hormone is secreted during one of the main sleep phases. The general sleep pattern can be broken down into two main periods, that of Slow Wave Sleep (SWS) and Rapid Eye Movement (REM).

During SWS the human body and brain shows little signs of being influenced by its environment and what is going on around it. In REM sleep there is a similar lack of response to the environment, but the brain activity is the same as that when awake. This is when dreams occur. REM sleep lasts for around 30 minutes and occurs every 90 minutes or so.

You may be surprised to learn that you dream around five times a night and for half an hour each time. That is because the dreams are not stored in the conscious part of the brain. The only ones which we seem able to recall are when REM sleep is disturbed for some reason. That means, you only remember the dreams you were having when you were woken up. You may only have woken for an instant, but you should be able to remember that dream.

A recurring theme of dreams is the prediction of the future

The significance of dreams are still not fully understood. The subject has fascinated scientists and scholars for years. Many great philosophers have also tried to explain dreams. It is known, however, that dreams have special meaning to the person who is having the dream.

One recurring theme of dreams seems to be prediction of the future. How many times have you heard someone say "I dreamt that would happen!" Maybe you have had such an experience yourself. Have you ever dreamt of walking or talking to a relative living overseas. Next day you receive a phone call out of the blue from that relative!

Dreams are also thought by some to be responsible for occurrences commonly called a "déjà vu". This is when you are sure you have witnessed or experienced an event before. When the event happens you have a strange feeling and try to think where or when it has happened before.

These feelings and the phenomena of déjà vu are important when it comes to lotteries. Wouldn't it be great if you could simply go to sleep and dream the winning numbers in a lottery! Unfortunately, dreams don't usually work in such a manner. That's not to say it never happens.

In January 1994 an Irish grandmother had a dream that she had won the lottery. In February, she did just that, becoming the country's second richest lottery winner ever!

DREAM WINNERS

Picking up her cheque for £2,916731 Mrs Mary Hayes, from County Wicklow in the Irish Republic, said, "Three weeks ago I dreamed that I had won the lottery and that I was collecting my cheque. I told my son about the dream and we had a bit of a joke about it."

Mary had been up against stiff opposition. The size of the jackpot had prompted nearly every household in the country to have a flutter. At the peak times, retailers were handling 8,000 entries per minute.

Mrs Hayes became the Republic's 19th Lottery Millionaire with her £1 bet, correctly choosing all six numbers. Earlier in August 1993, a housewife living in Co Galaway had taken home £3,031,527.

Newspapers also reported the case of Michael Gabriele from New Jersey in the USA. On holiday in Florida, Michael was trying to put behind him the recent death of his daughter in a climbing accident. In a dream, he recalled his daughter saying, "I'd like to bring you a little happiness, why not play the numbers?"

Following that dream, Michael remembered they had found a lottery ticket in his daughters car when the accident occurred. After talking it over with his wife, he played the numbers. Days later they were extremely wealthy.

INSTANT SAVER

When 22 year-old Australian Andrew Stevens asked his bank manager for a loan to buy a car he received a lecture on the virtues of saving. Two weeks later he watched the managers jaw hit the floor as he handed over a cheque for $25,000. Between his two visits he had won a first prize in 'Camelot cash' instant scratchcard game.

"I really took my manager's message to heart," said Andrew, "But I never expected such a good start to my new career as a saver."

But Andrew isn't planning on leaving all his winnings in the bank. "I think my 1982 Chevrolet deserves an up-grade and a new motor," he laughed, "I'll still have plenty left over though and my bank manager will be proud of me."

DOMINANT NUMBERS

If you are lucky you will have a dream just like Mary Hayes. More likely, though, is that you will have a dream that dominates and occurs in other dreams.

In other words part of a dream will appear in many other dreams. Say for example, you could dream about walking down the street, wearing a yellow jumper. You turn into the shop and meet a friend called Dave. The next night you may dream of being sat next to Dave on a plane on the way to the Seychelles. Again you are wearing a yellow jumper. On the third night you might be sat on a sandy beach in baking hot sun. Yet, again, for some reason you are wearing a yellow jumper. This is a case of a yellow jumper dominating dreams.

These dominating factors have even more significance to your life.

Dream experts have made catalogues of people's dreams and the dominating factors. These factors have then been compared to events that happened to the dream subjects and their lives at the time of the dreaming. Many psychological effects can be tracked in this manner and people's lives have been improved as a result.

Although it is often difficult to determine which item is significant in a dominant dream - is it the jumper that is important or the colour yellow? - dreams can be tabulated. One of these tabulations involves the relationship of dominant dreams and numbers.

NUMERICAL MEANINGS OF DREAMS

Listed here are the meanings of dreams in terms of numbers. If you catalogue your dreams and translate them into numbers, you may find one or more numbers dominating. Make a note of these and use them in your lottery entries.

You may dream, on separate nights of an absent lover, travelling on a plane and talking to a close friend. From the following table you will see that the number 18 is associated with each of these dreams. This would be termed a Dominant Number and should be used in your lottery entries, It may even be worth considering using it as your Key Number.

Absent sweetheart: 14, 18, 13, 9, 4.
Absent wife: 14, 5, 16, 7, 41.
Absent husband: 13, 4, 10, 6, 16
Absent friend: 14, 5, 7, 44, 46.
Accident involving a train: 7, 9, 11, 13.
Accident involving a plane: 10, 1, 44, 42, 5.
Accident involving an auto: 9, 44, 41, 45, 2.
Accident involving a fall: 11, 2, 8, 44, 43.
Address of an old friend: 10, 1, 13, 6, 20.
Address for a business: 5, 13, 31, 4, 11.

Address for your mother: 3, 2, 21, 12,
Address of a friend: 11, 2, 13, 37, 31.
Address of a sweetheart: 9, 16, 2, 7, 34.
Advice from a policeman: 5, 3, 23, 15, 32.
Advice from a friend: 7, 13, 33, 4, 8
Advice from your mother: 2, 4, 22, 26,
Advice from a sweetheart: 16, 12, 9, 13, 22.
Advice from a lawyer: 18, 19, 13, 12, 34.
Advice from your father: 9, 13, 4, 5, 34.
Advice from your sister: 19, 10, 12, 15, 27.
Afraid of water: 12, 3, 16, 6, 37.
Afraid of darkness: 5, 12, 21, 3, 39.
Ambulance ride: 6, 13, 21, 4, 43.
Ambulance wreck: 21, 3, 14, 15, 31.
Ambulance accident: 6, 2, 24, 26, 42.
Argument with wife: 21, 3, 14, 15, 32.
Argument with friend: 22, 4, 16, 14, 30.
Argument with husband: 18, 9, 14, 12, 35.
Argument with sweetheart: 15, 6, 16, 9, 24.
Baby sick: 8, 7, 1, 16, 32.
Baby sleeping:16, 7, 10, 1, 14.
Baby talking: 17, 8, 36, 14, 40.
Baby crying: 6, 10, 15, 5, 36.
Beautiful woman: 8, 35, 23, 32, 3.
Beautiful man: 8, 16, 11, 2, 37.
Birth of a baby: 7, 22, 32, 23, 5.
Child crying: 13, 15, 17, 4, 36.
Child sick: 7, 21, 14, 41, 12.
Child laughing: 22, 4, 16, 14, 36.
Crying man: 14, 5, 45, 10, 29.
Crying sweetheart: 18, 9, 10, 8, 38.
Crying sister: 21, 3, 15, 14, 32.
Death of a mother: 14, 5, 41, 13, 49.
Death of a friend: 22, 4, 49, 9, 13.
Death of relatives: 20, 2, 12, 13, 21.
Dentist pulling teeth: 16, 43, 49, 7, 34.
Divorce from wife: 16, 7, 10, 11, 44.
Divorce from husband: 9, 32, 24, 42, 23.

Dog playing: 14, 5, 18, 9, 46.
Dog barking: 10, 1, 19, 9, 39.
Dress, old: 14, 5, 41, 9, 28.
Dress, new: 18, 9, 27, 36, 45.
Eating at home: 14, 5, 36, 11, 41.
Eating dinner: 16, 7, 37, 6, 3.
Eating with sweetheart: 19, 10, 8, 5, 11.
Falling off high building: 17, 8, 16, 7, 32.
Falling out of bed: 16, 7, 10, 11, 28.
Falling out of a Window: 10, 20, 2, 13, 11.
Father, old: 19, 10, 18, 1, 38.
Father sick: 18, 9, 12, 11, 32.
Father dead: 14, 5, 38, 33, 11.
Fear of snakes: 12, 3, 9, 6, 30.
Fear of dying: 22, 4, 10, 18, 32.
Fear of a man: 13, 4, 37, 33, 10.
Fear of suffocating: 17, 8, 11, 3, 39.
Fear of animals: 10, 1, 34, 33, 7.
Fighting man: 15, 6, 45, 9, 11.
Fighting animals: 11, 2, 21, 19, 43.
Friend crying: 9, 10, 35, 8, 12.
Friend, dead or dying: 18, 9, 25, 7, 8.
Friend, male: 19, 10, 46, 15, 1.
Friend, female: 21, 3, 12, 15, 30.
Friend, laughing: 25, 7, 18, 16, 41.
Funeral, yours: 23, 5, 15, 14, 33.
Funeral, mother: 10, 1, 3, 7, 21.
Funeral, sister: 24, 6, 18, 15, 38.
Funeral, father: 27, 9, 18, 1, 28.
Funeral, brother: 13, 4, 24, 27,
Funeral, baby: 12, 3, 30, 39, 11.
Gun, shooting: 24, 6, 18, 15, 33,
Gun, shot by: 7, 25, 5, 20, 32.
Hair loss: 10, 1, 20, 8, 2.
Hands: 13, 4, 39, 31, 3.
Hat: 10, 1, 28, 8, 47.
Hospital: 19, 10, 1, 14, 12.
Hotel: 17, 8, 9, 32, 41.

Husband, sick: 14, 5, 19, 41, 18.
Husband, dead: 7, 31, 33, 4, 6.
Ice cream: 10, 1, 5, 18, 32.
Italy: 14, 5, 6, 8, 33.
Jail: 9, 6, 33, 3, 42.
Job, a new one: 12, 3, 17, 47, 41.
Job, an old one: 21, 3, 14, 7, 44.
Job, losing one: 16, 7, 10, 12, 45.
Journey over water: 18, 9, 47, 11, 14.
Journey by auto: 2, 10, 11, 23, 46.
Journey by air: 9, 10, 18, 1, 38
Keys, lost: 6, 10, 5, 15, 36.
Keys, found: 11, 2, 12, 18, 42.
Kissing: 17, 8, 9, 18, 38.
Kissing a baby: 9, 31, 35, 48.
Kissing sweetheart: 17, 8, 11, 12, 48.
Kissing another man's wife: 22, 4, 14, 16, 34.
Kissing another woman's husband: 17, 8, 13, 9, 46.
Kissing a woman: 15, 6, 8, 12, 42,
Kissing a man: 22, 4, 13, 14, 43.
Laughing: 20, 2, 11, 14, 47.
Letter: 20, 2, 13, 7, 6, 48,
Love affair with a friend: 14, 5, 7, 26, 38.
Love affair with different race: 8, 6, 12, 3, 29.
Love affair with a stranger: 10, 1, 21, 17, 12, 40.
Love affair at a party: 11, 2, 29, 31, 42.
Love in bed: 17, 8, 37, 10, 14.
Love in car: 22, 4, 14, 15, 38.
Love on a couch: 23, 5, 16, 14, 30.
Man: 16, 7, 36, 1, 29.
Marriage, yours: 15, 6, 27, 26, 8.
Marriage, broken: 13, 4, 35, 10, 45.
Medicine: 9, 15, 35, 6, 41.
Money, found: 12, 3, 6, 21, 42.
Money, lost: 10, 1, 25, 35, 7.
Money, stolen: 14, 5, 36, 35, 9.
Mother angry: 14, 5, 35, 11, 46.
Mother laughing: 8, 18, 9, 27.

COPY THAT

Staff of the photocopier company Xerox were toasting a nice 'little' dividend of £100,000 when their £2 ticket came up. The 19 members of a syndicate all work in the credit ratings department, and each will receive more than £5,000 - helping to improve their own credit ratings!

One member of the syndicate says he will now be able to go to his brother's 50th wedding celebrations in Malta. Another is sending for travel brochures to see if her first overseas trip will be to New York or into deepest Africa. One, a lover of the good life, is investing in a cellar full of premium red wines. While the joker of the syndicate claimed he was going to install a hot water spa in his dog's kennel!

Mother crying: 11, 2, 35, 8, 43.
Mother-in-law: 8, 31, 43, 34, 4.
Murder: 4, 49, 9, 32, 10
Naked in street: 15, 6, 38, 43, 34.
Naked in bed: 22, 4, 17, 13, 34.
Naked man: 15, 6, 26, 13, 39.
Naked woman: 3, 12, 20, 21, 41.
Naked in bath or shower: 17, 8, 9, 26, 35.
Night: 14, 5, 16, 7, 13.
Old man: 15, 6, 8, 7, 31.
Old woman: 10, 1, 32, 35.
Old people fighting: 8, 20, 26, 2, 48.
Operation: 10, 1, 22, 26, 48
Plane crash: 19, 10, 12, 15, 27
Plane on fire: 4, 12, 11, 13, 8.
Plane falling: 8, 13, 4, 34, 7.
Plane passenger: 20, 2, 14, 5, 41.
Plane landing: 10, 1, 7, 3, 21.
Plants: 16, 7, 36, 37, 9.

Police: 17, 8, 36, 38,
Ring, lost: 8, 21, 25, 12, 37.
Ring, found: 16, 7, 9, 32, 41.
River: 15, 6, 37, 35, 10.
Robbery: 18, 9, 13, 12, 34.
School: 7, 12, 5, 3, 27.
Scream for help: 19, 10, 14, 12, 5.
Screaming men: 25, 16, 7, 26, 6.
Screaming women: 7, 16, 23, 39, 30.
Screaming for police: 12, 3, 15, 10, 37.
Screaming child: 11, 2, 38, 3,
Shaving: 17, 8, 9, 34, 43.
Sickness: 11, 2, 10, 19, 43.
Sister: 10, 1, 41, 45, 9.
Sister-in-law: 40, 24, 42, 6, 48.
Sister, fighting with: 22, 4, 13, 15, 32.
Sister married: 16, 7, 25, 29, 14.
Sister sick: 7, 1, 16, 6, 39.
Sister dead: 21, 3, 12, 15, 30.
Sleep: 6, 1, 10, 5, 21.
Smoke: 9, 31, 35, 13, 8.
Snake: 13, 23, 38, 11, 5.
Special moments with friends: 8, 20, 26, 29.
Storm: 17, 8, 12, 5, 42.
Stranger, woman: 13, 4, 17, 12, 46.
Stranger, young: 5, 30, 20, 23. 32.
Stranger, old: 8, 20, 26. 6, 2.
Stranger, dead: 13, 4, 16, 6, 41.
Stranger, sick: 9, 27, 20, 2, 7.
Swimming: 4, 20, 22, 2, 48.
Talking: 10, 1, 35, 23, 32.
Talking in your sleep: 11, 2, 19, 10, 42.
Talking to husband: 9, 25, 22, 7, 38.
Talking to dead: 11, 2, 20, 29, 49.
Talking to wife: 13, 4, 8, 5, 30.
Talking to friend: 19, 10, 9, 18, 37.
Talking to sweetheart: 8, 21, 15, 25, 12.
Talking to animals: 15, 6, 26, 25, 13.

Telephone: 4, 13, 31, 10, 41.
Toothache: 3, 20, 21, 10, 12.
Travel, especially to exotic places: 4, 31, 40, 43.
Travelling through space: 7, 17, 34, 37, 10
Visit from friends: 10, 1, 28, 44, 8.
Visit from in-laws: 6, 15, 5, 26, 46.
Visit to a hospital: 2, 1, 11, 14, 28.
Walking: 3, 11, 1, 14, 29.
Wedding, yours: 27, 9, 36, 45, 3.
Wedding of a friend: 17, 8, 28, 15, 10.
Winning money: 9, 33, 3, 45, 48.
Winning lottery: 18, 9, 17, 8, 35.
Working: 12, 3, 44, 4, 48.
Writing a letter: 15, 6, 10, 5, 36.
Xmas: 6, 22, 28, 11, 2.
Xmas Eve: 16, 7, 19, 15, 41.
Xmas card: 4, 22, 2, 26,
Xmas night: 3, 21, 12, 2, 37.
Xmas gift: 4, 11, 21, 3.
Xmas tree: 8, 34, 41, 14, 48.
Xmas day: 9, 42, 34, 32, 43.
Zoo: 12, 3, 6, 33, 42.

TIME AND AGAIN

You could be forgiven in thinking one lottery win is all you could hope for in your life. But there are plenty of cases of people who have won on several occasions. Recently a small businessman from Caringbah in Australia who calls himself 'Mr Lucky' has pocketed $100,000 only four years after winning a similar amount.

"Sure I buy a lot of tickets, but it's been a great investment - I'm miles ahead," he said when talking about his latest win. Walking away with a smile on his face, he also admitted that he had won a 'miserly' $25,000 last year!

Similarly a Tamworth woman won $100,000 in the lottery nearly 40 years after she last picked up a major prize. Back in the 50's she won a third prize equivalent to $20,000 today. "In those days you could buy a house for $30,000 so it was a big win."

Although Mr Jones didn't have to wait so long, his last win was recorded in 1971 when he accepted a cheque for $60,000. Now in his 83rd year, Mr Jones has won a third prize of $5,000 which he plans to spend making his 1972 model Cortina roadworthy again.

However, none of the above players can match Tom Briggs for his number of smaller wins. Tom, a freelance journalist first won $10,000 on an instant-win scratchcard. Then things went quiet for 8 years until he picked up another $5,000 on the same scratchcard game. Two more years passed before a further $10,000 dropped into Toms bank account. And to continue his run of good luck, Tom has just won $4,400 on the lottery.

"All my lucky strikes have been very timely," said Tom, "And this one is no exception."

9 ALPHANUMERIC SYSTEMS

An alphanumeric system is one which allows you to translate letters into numbers.

The Mystic Chart already discussed in an earlier chapter is an alphanumeric chart. This changes letters into one of the numbers from 1 to 9.

This is the Mystic Chart:

1	2	3	4	5	6	7	8	9
A	B	C	D	E	F	G	H	I
J	K	L	M	N	O	P	Q	R
S	T	U	V	W	X	Y	Z	

If you remember you used it to translate Albert Einstein into:

A	L	B	E	R	T	E	I	N	S	T	E	I	N
1	3	2	5	9	2	5	9	5	1	2	5	9	5

This was achieved by replacing the letters with the number at the top of the columns containing that letter.

There are many other alphanumeric systems and the following sections detail a few of the more popular. As you become familiar with each system return to the section on the Mystic Chart to remind yourself on how to apply the numbers once you've derived them from the chart.

PROGRESSIVE LETTERS

This has to be one of the simplest alphanumeric systems on the go. It relies simply on translating the letter into a number corresponding to its position in the alphabet.

1	2	3	4	5	6	7	8	9	10
A	B	C	D	E	F	G	H	I	J

11	12	13	14	15	16	17	18	19	20
K	L	M	N	O	P	Q	R	S	T

21	22	23	24	25	26
U	V	W	X	Y	Z

Have go at translating "I feel lucky." You should get the simple number sequence:

$$9\ 6\ 5\ 5\ 12\ 12\ 21\ 3\ 11\ 25$$

Since even simple sentences produce a large set of numbers using the Progressive Letter System, you can afford to simply discard any duplicated numbers. Also, since each letter corresponds to a number between 1 and 26, you know none are going to fall out of the required range. You get:

$$9,\ 6,\ 5,\ 12,\ 21,\ 3,\ 11\ \&\ 25$$

Play three of these numbers in Pick 3, four in Pick 4, six of these numbers in the lotto or use them all in a wheel system entry.

THE PYRAMID

The Pyramid Table works in much the same way as the Mystic Chart. However, the letters are arranged in a different order.

1	2	3	4	5	6	7	8	9
A	H	E	O	F	Y	M	D	R
	Q	T	U	I	P	S	G	
		W	J	K	L	Z		
			X	C	V	B		
				N				

You can translate anything using these tables, not just names. You could translate the name of your road for instance. The address 15 Primrose Mount becomes:

15 69579473 74453

Taking these as pairs of numbers we get:

15, 69, 57, 94, 73, 74, 45, 3

Reversing digits where the number is out of range gives:

15, 96, 75, 49, 37, 47, 45, 3

Then adding digits for numbers which are still out of range or duplicated:

15, 14, 12, 49, 37, 47, 45, 3

Leaving eight numbers with which to play the lottery, in say an Eight Number (8 game) Wheel.

NEVER GIVE UP

Within days of arriving in Australia as an immigrant during 1952, Dutch-born Corrie de Boer bought her first lottery ticket. She listened intently to the draw on the radio and was 'shattered' when her number failed to come up. Nevertheless, Corrie continued to play and had to wait over 41 years for her first win. Picking up her cheque for £50,000 in an instant win game, Corrie confirmed that perseverance certainly pays off.

THE BACON SIZZLER

Viscount Francis Bacon was a famous statesman, scientist and philosopher born in London during 1561. He was one of the first people to start using codes for fun. Viscount Bacon was knighted when he came to parliament and then imprisoned for accepting bribes. Later pardoned and released from jail, this is his code:

A	B	C	D	E	F	G	H	I
27	28	29	30	31	32	33	34	35

J	K	L	M	N	O	P	Q	R
0	10	11	12	13	14	15	16	17

S	T	U	V	W	X	Y	Z
18	19	20	0	21	22	23	24

So, Francis Bacon's own first name would translate as follows:

32, 17, 27, 13, 29, 35, 18

Again, all the numbers in this system are within the normall lottery range, so no reversal or digit adding should be necessary. Francis, who died a poor man, could either have played these seven numbers in a wheel, or discarded one to give him his six Sizzling Bacon Numbers.

ANCIENT TRIANGLES

Pythagoras (580-497 BC) is believed to be the 'grandfather' of numerology. While his peers were still sacrificing goats to appease the gods and alter the future, Pythagoras proposed the use of numbers to foretell what the future held.

In ancient times, such as those of Pythagoras, philosophers believed numbers had their own life. They believed that numbers evolved like any being and could carry their own life form through time.

Here is one of the ancient alphanumeric tables:

A	B	C	D	E	F	G	H	I
5	4	7	1	1	6	9	9	14

J	K	L	M	N	O	P	Q	R
22	14	9	16	24	13	16	21	21

S	T	U	V	W	X	Y	Z
7	5	4	23	15	13	4	4

The name Pythagoras becomes the number sequence:

$$16, 4, 5, 9, 5, 9, 13, 21, 5, 7$$

Dropping duplicates and putting in numerical order:

$$4, 5, 7, 9, 13, 16, 21$$

Another seven numbers which could make someone rich. Do you think Pythagoras would have been able to appreciate the size of some of the lottery prizes on offer these days?

REINVEST FOR RICHES

A modest £25 win on the instant win scratchcard didn't set a Linlithgow man's heart racing. So he decided to 'go for broke' with 25 tickets in the main lottery. One week later his pulse rate went through the roof. Not only did he win £50,000 as a first prize, but he also pocketed two £500 prizes for being one off the biggie plus a minor £5 for good measure.

10 THE ODDS AGAINST RUNNING A LOTTERY

Before the National Lottery could get off the ground in Britain, an operator had to be found. The Government wanted a company willing and able to take on the entire complex task of running a lottery. To be the successful bidder, they would have to show an ability to mix computer expertise with mass marketing skills and provide a vast network for ticket distribution.

To stand a chance of success, the company would need to set up their computer network within six months, appoint over 40,000 retail outlets with machinery to handle entries and be able to cope with 3,000 entries per second at peak times.

An estimated £100 million annual profit for the winner

Why would any company want to take on such an onerous task? Well, the estimated £100 million annual profit forecasts may have had something to do with it!

Eight main contenders finally surfaced in the run up to a winner being announced in May 1994. If one had been selected by chance, they would each have had odds against being picked of 1:8. However, the judges were taking just a little more into account - especially with the farce of 1826 stuck in their minds. Each applicant was required to submit 20 copies of their application detailing how they would run the enterprise. Camelot's application alone weighed in at a massive 7,000 pages.

William Hill, the high street bookies were giving the following odds against being picked to run the lottery:

The UK Lottery Foundation	7/2 (favourite)
Great British Lottery Company	4/1
Camelot	9/2
NM Rothschild and Tattersalls	5/1
The Enterprise Lottery	11/2
Games for Good Causes	6/1
Lotco	6/1
Rainbow	20/1

A SMASHING TIME

Six young glaziers were hell bent on celebrating their lottery win to the full. Starting with a champagne breakfast, the six hired a chauffeur-driven limousine to pick up their cheque for £133,609.68.

"Our business has suffered more than most through the recession so we've got every right to live it up," said the syndicate leader and owner of the company. "We only started entering six months ago," he added, "And it will certainly put a smile back on to my bank manager's face."

The UK Lottery Foundation

The media's favourite, spurred on by a promise to return all profits to a charity called The Lottery Foundation.

Headed by the gifted self-publicist Richard Branson and Lord Young, a former Trade Minister, this bid generated huge public interest because of the non-profit motive. IBM were put forward to provide the computer equipment and Mars were touted as the distribution experts with a link to small retailers. The bid indicated that, if successful, Lords Whitelaw and Tonypandy would be the charity's trustees.

The downside of this bid was considered to be the consortium's complete lack of practical experience. Also, influential suits in the city believed the lack of profit motive would lead to the business not realising its full potential.

Great British Lottery Company

This consortium was dominated by media companies like Granada TV, Vodafone, Carlton Communications and Associated Newspapers. The group was chaired by Granada's chief executive Gerry Robinson.

Adding weight to the financial and security side of the bid were two well known names. Hambros Bank joined the consortium as did Sir Kenneth Newman a former Metropolitan police commissionaire.

Reports calculate that the group spent around £2.5 million on their bid.

NM Rothschild and Tatteralls

NM Rothschild is a large merchant bank used to handling large amounts of money. They also had good government connections. Tattersalls is a company with experience in running the Australian lottery. This group's campaign was fairly low-key.

The Enterprise Lottery

The leader of this consortium was the Tote, bringing gambling expertise. Others in the

GRATEFUL DAD

A Filipino refrigeration workers' little boy was taken seriously ill nearly 15 years ago. "The Children's Hospital saved my boy's life and I said then that I would make a donation to the hospital as soon as I could afford it. That time has come," he said. And as sole winner of THREE MILLION in the Father's Day draw he can afford a hefty donation. The windfall means security for life for the entire family.

group included the electrical company GEC, entertainments experts Thorn EMI, and Lord Wyatt.

The Tote was established by parliament in 1963 and it was only ever intended to cover horse racing. This could have counted against the consortium.

Games for Good Causes

An early strong contender with the hotel and gambling group Ladbrokes, the merchant bank Kleinwort Benson and TV company Meridian. The technological back-up came from the direction of American firms AT&T and NCR.

Malcolm Brookes headed the bid as chief of Vernons, the pools company owned by Ladbrokes.

Lotco

Led by the Rank Organisation which runs hundreds of bingo halls around the country. Ian Neilson was the resident expert and proposed chief executive. Neilson had experience running Canada's largest lottery in Ontario.

Rainbow

Rank outsider. Headed by Sir Patrick Sheehy, the chairman of BAT industries, it also embraced the advertising company Leo Burnett. The group did not have any expertise in computer technology and admitted it would have to contract out that part of the operation. They hoped to enlist the help of one of the pools companies.

Camelot

The last, and ultimately successful consortium were known simply as Camelot, as indeed they still are. Cadbury Schweppes joined forces with Racal Electronics, Gtech, De La Rue and ICL. Each company held a 22.5% stake in Camelot, apart from ICL who only held 10%.

Cadbury brought to the group expertise in consumer marketing as well as a wide distribution base which already reached to corner-shops, newsagents and supermarkets. With sales of around £3.7 billion from more than 170 countries, Cadbury Schweppes is a well established member of the Footsie 100.

Racal Electronics provided the technological back-up for the huge undertaking of linking up 10,000 computerised outlets in just over five months and 35,000 by the end of the century. Racal had a strong hand since its system already linked 150,000 gov-

200,000 man-hours were spent producing the 7,000 page bid document

ernment users on a national data network. Racal's sales, prior to the lottery, were around £1 billion.

De La Rue is the world's largest supplier of security printing, including cash handling equipment and bank notes. This made them an ideal qualifier for the printing of 'instant win' scratchcards. A profit of £100 million in 1993 was earned by 7,600 employees worldwide. It had supplied other lotteries for 20 years prior to the bid.

Gtech contributed experience from the USA. As a designer, manufacturer and installer of systems it already supported 62 existing lottery structures for Governments in five continents.

ICL held the smaller stake. They were the leading supplier of point-of-sale equipment in Britain. ICL's annual sales revenue before the lottery was around £2.6 billion.

The consortium spent two years and 200,000 man-hours working on their bid because they expected it to become the biggest in the world. All that work showed in the impressive 7,000 page application it delivered to the authorities. In total Camelot delivered more than half a tonne of paper for its application.

The probity of each partner in the consortium came under intense scrutiny. Even MI5 were involved in the investigation, especially since rumours surfaced about Gtech's links with the American mafia.

FLAT BROKE

Dustbin-man Warren Smith described himself as 'Flat Broke' when a work accident left him with a smashed ankle for more than a year. Unable to work and living in a Housing Association, Warren was surviving on the dole. Then his situation changed overnight with a £50,000 win on the lottery. "I'm not able to do physical work any more. And I can't run, even though I used to love running. But now, maybe I'll be able to do something with my life again," said Warren.

APPENDIX A

COMBINATIONS

The first column gives the number of articles from which the first row are to be taken. For example, if you are to take 6 numbers from 49 possible numbers in a lottery, go down the first column to '49', and then across to the column headed '6'. The number of combinations of 6 numbers from 49 possible is 13,983,816.

	2	3	4	5	6	7	8	9	10
3	3	1							
4	6	4	1						
5	10	10	5	1					
6	15	20	15	6	1				
7	21	35	35	21	7	1			
8	28	56	70	56	28	8	1		
9	36	84	126	126	84	36	9	1	
10	45	120	210	252	210	120	45	10	1
11	55	165	330	462	462	330	165	55	11
12	66	220	495	792	924	792	495	220	66
13	78	286	715	1287	1716	1716	1287	715	286
14	91	364	1001	2002	3003	3432	3003	2002	1001
15	105	455	1365	3003	5005	6435	6435	5005	3003
16	120	560	1820	4368	8008	11440	12870	11440	8008
17	136	680	2380	6188	12376	19448	24310	24310	19448
18	153	816	3060	8568	18564	31824	43758	48620	43758
19	171	969	3876	11628	27132	50388	75582	92378	92378
20	190	1140	4845	15504	38760	77520	125970	167960	184756
21	210	1330	5985	20349	54264	116280	203490	293930	352716
22	231	1540	7315	26334	74613	170544	319770	497420	646646
23	253	1771	8855	33649	100947	245157	490314	817190	1144066
24	276	2024	10626	42504	134596	346104	735471	1307504	1961256
25	300	2300	12650	53130	177100	480700	1081575	2042975	3268760
26	325	2600	14950	65780	230230	657800	1562275	3124550	5311735

	2	3	4	5	6	7	8	9	10
27	351	2925	17550	80730	296010	888030	2220075	4686825	8436285
28	378	3276	20475	98280	376740	1184040	3108105	6906900	13123110
29	406	3654	23751	118755	475020	1560780	4292145	10015005	20030010
30	435	4060	27405	142506	593775	2035800	5852925	14307150	30045015
31	465	4495	31465	169911	736281	2629575	7888725	20160075	44352165
32	496	4960	35960	201376	906192	3365856	10518300	28048800	64512240
33	528	5456	40920	237336	1107568	4272048	13884156	38567100	92561040
34	561	5984	46376	278256	1344904	5379616	18156204	52451256	1.31E+08
35	595	6545	52360	324632	1623160	6724520	23535820	70607460	1.84E+08
36	630	7140	58905	376992	1947792	8347680	30260340	94143280	2.54E+08
37	666	7770	66045	435897	2324784	10295472	38608020	1.24E+08	3.48E+08
38	703	8436	73815	501942	2760681	12620256	48903492	1.63E+08	4.73E+08
39	741	9139	82251	575757	3262623	15380937	61523748	2.12E+08	6.36E+08
40	780	9880	91390	658008	3838380	18643560	76904685	2.73E+08	8.48E+08
41	820	10660	101270	749398	4496388	22481940	95548245	3.5E+08	1.12E+09
42	861	11480	111930	850668	5245786	26978328	1.18E+08	4.46E+08	1.47E+09
43	903	12341	123410	962598	6096454	32224114	1.45E+08	5.64E+08	1.92E+09
44	946	13244	135751	1086008	7059052	38320568	1.77E+08	7.09E+08	2.48E+09
45	990	14190	148995	1221759	8145060	45379620	2.16E+08	8.86E+08	3.19E+09
46	1035	15180	163185	1370754	9366819	53524680	2.61E+08	1.1E+09	4.08E+09
47	1081	16215	178365	1533939	10737573	62891499	3.14E+08	1.36E+09	5.18E+09
48	1128	17296	194580	1712304	12271512	73629072	3.77E+08	1.68E+09	6.54E+09
49	1176	18424	211876	1906884	**<u>13983816</u>**	85900584	4.51E+08	2.05E+09	8.22E+09
50	1225	19600	230300	2118760	15890700	99884400	5.37E+08	2.51E+09	1.03E+10
51	1275	20825	249900	2349060	18009460	1.16E+08	6.37E+08	3.04E+09	1.28E+10
52	1326	22100	270725	2598960	20358520	1.34E+08	7.53E+08	3.68E+09	1.58E+10
53	1378	23426	292825	2869685	22957480	1.54E+08	8.86E+08	4.43E+09	1.95E+10
54	1431	24804	316251	3162510	25827165	1.77E+08	1.04E+09	5.32E+09	2.39E+10
55	1485	26235	341055	3478761	28989675	2.03E+08	1.22E+09	6.36E+09	2.92E+10
56	1540	27720	367290	3819816	32468436	2.32E+08	1.42E+09	7.58E+09	3.56E+10

APPENDIX B

Eight Number Wheel (16 games)
with one Key Number (KN)

KN	1	2	3	4	5
KN	1	2	3	4	6
KN	1	2	3	4	7
KN	1	2	3	5	6
KN	1	2	3	5	7
KN	1	2	3	6	7
KN	1	2	4	5	6
KN	1	2	4	5	7
KN	1	2	4	6	7
KN	1	2	5	6	7
KN	1	3	4	5	6
KN	1	3	4	5	7
KN	1	3	4	6	7
KN	1	3	5	6	7
KN	1	4	5	6	7
KN	2	3	4	5	6

Seven Number Wheel (16 games)
with two Key Numbers

KN	KN	1	2	3	4
KN	KN	1	2	3	5
KN	KN	1	2	3	6
KN	KN	1	2	3	7
KN	KN	1	2	4	5
KN	KN	1	2	4	6
KN	KN	1	2	4	7
KN	KN	1	2	5	6
KN	KN	1	2	5	7
KN	KN	1	3	4	5

KN	KN	1	3	4	6
KN	KN	1	3	4	7
KN	KN	1	4	5	6
KN	KN	1	4	5	7
KN	KN	2	3	4	5
KN	KN	2	3	4	6

Ten Number Wheel (10 games)

1	2	3	4	5	6
1	2	3	4	7	8
1	2	3	4	9	10
1	2	5	6	7	8
1	2	5	6	9	10
1	2	7	8	9	10
3	4	5	6	7	8
3	4	5	6	9	10
3	4	7	8	9	10
5	6	7	8	9	10

Nine Number Wheel (6 games)

1	2	3	4	5	6
1	2	3	4	5	7
1	2	3	4	5	8
1	2	6	7	8	9
1	3	5	6	7	8
2	4	6	7	8	9

Nine Number Wheel (9 games)

1	2	3	4	5	6
1	2	3	4	5	7
1	2	3	4	5	8
1	2	6	7	8	9
1	3	5	6	7	8
2	4	6	7	8	9
3	4	6	7	8	9
3	5	6	7	8	9
4	5	6	7	8	9

Nine Number Wheel (12 games)

1	2	3	4	5	6
1	2	3	4	5	7
1	2	3	4	5	8
1	2	6	7	8	9
1	3	5	6	7	8
1	3	5	6	8	9
1	4	5	6	8	9
2	3	4	6	7	8
2	4	6	7	8	9
3	4	6	7	8	9
3	5	6	7	8	9
4	5	6	7	8	9

APPENDIX C

POINTS TO REMEMBER

①   Make sure you enter in plenty of time. Queues can form when the deadline draws near.

②   Take great care when filling in your entry slip.

③   Check the numbers given back to you by the lottery company. Make sure they are the numbers you wish to enter, and ensure no mistakes have been made.

④   Do not bet with more money than you can afford. Your odds of winning are low, so be prepared to lose the money you are wagering. A rule of thumb is to never bet more than 1% of your salary.

⑤   Never play the lottery on credit.

⑥   It is better to play the lottery on your own. If you wish to form a syndicate, only join one with people you know and can trust. If you are serious about your entries, get a contract drawn up between all syndicate members. Make sure all of your members are complying with point four.

⑦   Try to establish a routine with your entries. Make sure you play regularly, within the boundaries of point three.

⑧   Do not tell anyone the numbers you are playing with. Even subconsciously, someone else could use one or two of the numbers from your selection, lowering your potential winnings.

⑨   Keep your tickets in a safe place before the draw is made.

⑩   Do not forget to check your tickets.

And finally...   If you've got a winner of any sort, don't let it out of your sight until you've got the prize money!!!

Appendix D

Winspiration

If ever you get fed up and find yourself in need of some inspiration to help you win that elusive million, take a read through some of these lucky winner stories. Perhaps there is a clue or two hidding in some of them!

RUGBY LEAGUE BET

A small time bet on the outcome of a Rugby League game turned up trump for two workmates from Windsor. The loser had to fork out for a couple o instant win lottery tickets. It was the best bet the friends will ever make be cause it netted them a cool £250,000 with a top of the range win. Both win ners work in the same bank and they both applied bankers logic to their pros pects. "It's equivalent to 25 years' savings after tax," said one, "So I'll pay off my mortgage."

NO RUSH

The winners of big lottery prizes usually can't wait to lay their hands on the money. Most swoop on the lottery representative and stay there until the cheque is handed over. Not so one small businessman and winner o £50,000. He was aware of his win for more than 11 months before he turned up and claimed his winnings.

"I didn't really need the money," said the lucky winner, "So I left it with the lottery company which was as good as putting it in the bank. It was a sort o family fund." The winner has four children. "Now I've got some busines plans which need financial backing and the children's education is beginning to reach an expensive stage. So I thought I would claim my prize!"

MOTHER'S MOTORBIKE

A Harley Davidson motorcycle was top of the list for an Australian mother of two teenagers who won $100,000.

"I just couldn't come to terms with suddenly coming into that sort of money," she said, "It would be great to have a brand new Harley Davidson to replace the 1980 Yamaha I'm pushing around now."

GOLFING PROS

Four golfing friends didn't know they were playing for a prize which would have gladdened the heart of any professional. The losers had to buy lottery tickets for the four and the 'trophy' converted to a prize of £50,000.

"We've often played for lottery tickets, but never before have they brought such dividends," the ticket holder said.

RETIRING WIN

A North Rocks woman tagged her lottery ticket "RETIRE" with the hope that she could win enough to enable her to give up work. When she won a prize of £51,000 in a jackpot lottery she said "I've been wanting to retire but couldn't afford to, this should do it!".

CABBIE CONGRATULATIONS

A recent £1,000,000 Lotto Clean Up draw promotion saw taxi driver Delfin from Kingsford do exactly that. He cleaned up on the first division and by playing a system 9 scored an extra £15,000 as well. Delfin, a 58 year old taxi driver said he "felt like a king" after being woken with the news. He was due to start a 3am shift but decided to take a sickie instead. He and his Spanish wife have a 26 year old son and a 21 year old daughter. "We'll take a holiday to Spain our first there in 16 years" he said. As a constant reminder of their Spanish roots Delfin plans to buy a hacienda on the Gold Coast so he can become one of the in-crowd. Their daughter has Down's Syndrome so his win will take a lot of pressure off the family as well.

SOLICITING A WIN

A long running punters syndicate in a solicitors office easily had its most spectacular result when one of the group scratched up an instant prize of £100,000. The five women in the syndicate have had only modest success with their punting investments. A £25 win on the horses was their previous best result.

Terrie Jones set a new standard for the group when she decided to punt the weekly kitty of £5 on two instant scratchies.

Terries magic touch came up trumps with a £100,000 dividend. It was timely as Kerrie had just announced her engagement. "What a great start this will give us" she said as she hurriedly phoned her fiancee.

Three of the group are married and home improvements are high on their list of priorities.

The youngest syndicate member, Gaynor, who is 21, will splurge out on a new car.

DUTCH HAPPINESS

Harry had been buying lottery tickets for eleven years. But there was never much of a win to write home about. Then he met his future wife, Noreen. At first he had trouble convincing her that it was worth the small weekly outlay. But he is of the opinion that "if you don't play you don't win". So Noreen had little choice but to play along. Shortly after, they took off the £50,000 prize in a Jackpot Lottery. This will be used to buy a house outside The Hague.

RAINY DAY

Life's road ahead is suddenly smoother for a young Grafton couple following a visit from Lady Luck.

Richie Watkins won £51,000 in a Jackpot Lottery. This event means he'll demolish his mortgage, acquire a much needed set of wheels and set aside something for a rainy day. "'What a difference a day makes" to coin a phrase" said Richie who works in the Parks and Gardens department of Grafton City Council.

"We're not destitute, but we're far from being silvertails. I can't believe we could be so lucky".

Richie's wife Brenda was at home with their two young sons (aged 3 and nine months) when the call from the Lotteries Office came through. When he said he had some information that Richie might welcome, she shot off on a tour of the parks to tell him the good news.

BIRTHDAY BONANZA

A young mother living in Beverley Hills received a £1 lottery ticket from her brother as a birthday gift.

It turned out to be a present worth £100,000 when she won first prize in a Jackpot Lottery.

With three young kids and plenty of mortgage this winner knows just how she is going to spend her windfall. Part of her prize she'll be giving to her brother who has bought some land.

SLAVE SALVER

A group of production workers who make life saving equipment won some live savers of their own in a Jackpot Lottery.

The syndicate has nine members in it and is called "Slaves".

The nine colleagues agree they will put their £100,000 win to conservative good use. Home improvements and mortgages will be high on the priority list for most of them. They intend to keep the syndicate going hoping to land a really big windfall.

SOAPSUDS

Two old friends who had worked together as cleaners for years shared a first prize of £49,000. They called their ticket 'Soapsuds' because "We were up to our elbows in Soapsuds for years" one explained.

Marilyn Walker and Jan Andersen have known each other for thirty years. Marilyn plans to spend her share of the prize in an attack on her mortgage which she and her husband took out on a house they bought only a couple of years ago. Jan and her husband are in a small business which will welcome an injection of funds.

NURSERY STYLE

A young rigger and his pregnant wife were looking for a second hand cot for their first child due in a couple of months. Then they won £503,000 in Lotto. "My wife gave up her job recently so making ends meet on one wage was proving tight" the rigger said. "We didn't know how we were going to cope when the baby arrived".

Now they plan to buy an up-market home with a proper nursery.

BIRTHDAY MAGIC

A 38-year old factory foreman from Minto and his 36-year old wife woke up to the news that they had won £500,000 on Lotto. Trevor and Wendy were sound asleep when Loto came calling as Trevor rises at 5am to go to work.

The couple then woke their three children to tell them that they will be able to finish painting the house, pay for renovations and buy a new car. Wendy has her eye on a diamond ring.

The couple had been playing Lotto for several years. They threw away their original numbers two months ago and chose this winning combination by using birthdays.

Trevor's workmates thought Trevor had won a few month's ago when he'd resigned from his job of 18 years. "It wasn't as exciting as that he said, I'd just been offered another job and taken it".

OK ON THE FARM

Local hairdresser Catherine Egan and Farmer David Goodwin shared first prize of £100,000 in a Jackpot lottery. The winning ticket was bought with money Catherine had given David for oats which he supplied for her daughter's pony.

"David didn't want to take the money and so agreed to spend it on Lottery tickets" said Catherine amid pandemonium as well wishers besieged her salon.

Catherine has four sons aged 11, 14, 16 and 18, so there are plenty of ideas around for how she should spend it.

As for David he has already used some of his winnings on the farm. He's bought a new truck and the cattle yards have had a face lift.

LIGHTNING STRIKES TWICE

Bill Phillips of Granville doesn't mind being called a "Double Dipper".

Back in 1991 he won £50,000 in a Jackpot Lottery and then 16 months later he won £50,000 again.

"I don't believe that lightning strikes twice in the same place" says Bill. "So I give myself every chance of maintaining my luck, I buy a Lottery ticket just about every day.

Bill, who lives with his parents is going to use this on their home, and look around for one of his own. His second winning ticket was marked 'Red Limit' which turned out to be the name of the first greyhound he'd raced some years ago.

NO APRIL FOOL

It was hard for the Lottery officials to prove their bona fides when they phoned winners on 1 April.

When the Lotterie's Jean Close identified herself to Julie Harris at the DPP's office in Newcastle, Julie was very sceptical indeed. It took a lot of talking to convince her that she and 14 of her colleagues had picked up a prize of £2,500. In fact they weren't convinced until they'd checked the numbers on the Lottery Hotline.

SENTIMENTAL JOURNEY HOME

Two brothers will be able to return home to Germany to see their brother who is dying. They won £50,000 in Jackpot Lottery. They scored their windfall with a free ticket they had received for being one off a prize in an earlier lottery. They plan to make their sentimental journey home to see their brother, with a sister as well.

GAME SET AND MATCH

Many rich memories are shared by a group of 15 friends who have been playing tennis together every Thursday for 35 years in Sydney.

One of their most memorable events occurred recently when the syndicate won £100,000. For some time they had been putting in 10p a week for Lottery tickets without a great deal of luck. That suddenly changed with this win and a prize of £500 for being one off the big prize with another ticket.

When the tennis club kicked off in the '50s most of the group were newly weds. Now there are more than 50 grandchildren. They also used to play for full day, now they are a bit more sedate, playing for just half a day.

They received their winners' cheque on a Thursday, after tennis and followed by a celebratory lunch.

NO FOOL

There's a car salesman in Moss Vale who is eligible for membership to the Sceptics Union.

He refused to accept a bank cheque in favour of a local man who was known in the district for being short of cash and less than honourable with his payments. The local man had ordered two top of the range new cars.

What the salesman didn't know was that the resident had won £1,000,000 in Lotto. So the buyer took his business elsewhere and the car salesman just sees red everytime the guy drives past.

HAPPY ANNIVERSARY

Wendy and Tony Jaconsen had a special wedding anniversary celebration boosted by a £9,000 win in Tele-Spin won by Tony.

After the show Tony said "It's our ninth wedding anniversary on Wednesday, we'll be able to make it a great celebration now". Wendy bought the winning scratchie for Tony, then went to Queensland on holiday. Tony surprised her by joining her to celebrate their anniversary in style. Tony, a self employed carpenter said the money would be spent to reduce their mortgage.

TOOTHACHE CURED

A Castle Hill school teacher left the dentist's chair to learn that he had won £250,000 in the Lottery.

Needless to say he was feeling no pain when told he had won first prize.

The Lotteries Office tracked him down to his dental appointment soon after the Lottery was drawn.

"If I wasn't feeling numb in the dentist's chair, I certainly am now" was his initial reaction.

GONE BUT NOT FORGOTTEN

80-year old Olive Shearer won second prize in a Lottery.

Olive believes her late husband may have had something to do with it.

Before he died, just over a year ago, the couple took lottery tickets together regularly. Olive has continued the investments on their joint registration card.

"This is great news" said Olive, "it will give me more independence".

NOT TOILET HUMOUR

From cleaning lady to quarter millionaire overnight is the fairy-tale story of Margaret Hamson from Singleton.

She shared £500,000 in Lotto with her sister, Beryl Robertson.

Margaret, a 39 year old mother of five, chose a novel location to discover her wealth.

She checked her numbers against the results whilst sitting on the toilet.

"I nearly had a heart attack" she said.

First item on her spending list is a home of her own. It will replace their rented council one where she lives with her husband and five children.

And of course there is an ever growing shopping list from the kids which includes a couple of motor bikes and a horse for starters.

THE NATIONAL LOTTERY MAGAZINE

Your chances of being STRUCK BY LIGHTNING are better than those of winning the lottery. BUT, you can improve your chances of being hit by lightning by standing in a thunderstorm and holding a metal rod. Likewise, you can **improve your chances of winning the lottery** by using techniques developed in America, Australia, Spain and many other countries with major lotteries.

The National Lottery Magazine brings you all the latest from the world of lotteries, with one express aim - to HELP YOU WIN THE LOTTERY. News, views, reviews, stories, lottery techniques, and tips all combine to give you what could be the winning edge in the MAIN NATIONAL LOTTERY and INSTANT SCRATCHIES.

STATISTICS EXPERTS will analyse the latest draws together with the numbers chosen by winners and losers alike.

Lottery BOOKS and COMPUTER SOFTWARE programmes are reviewed. Find out how useful they are before you buy. Are they easy to understand and how powerful are the techniques or routines incorporated?

Perhaps the most useful sections of *The National Lottery Magazine* will deal with the latest and most up-to-date techniques for gaining the upper hand. If a new method appears which can help you win, rest assured YOU WILL BE THE FIRST TO HEAR. And that is one of the main ADVANTAGES you can gain in a *pari-mutuel* game such as the lottery.

In each edition the LATEST WINNERS tell their stories. Apart from SHARING IN THEIR EXCITEMENT you can discover how they picked their numbers and see if you can use some of their ideas.

While the emphasis is on British lotteries, news from other OVERSEAS LOTTERIES will be analysed - including Germany, Spain and France. In particular, those lotteries from Europe which are easily entered from Britain will be reviewed. Are your odds better in other countries? How do their lotteries work and can you gain any advantage? Read *The National Lottery Magazine* for the answers!

Information on the most recent DEVELOPMENTS from the lottery companies. What are the latest games, and how do they work? What are the odds associated with each game, and which are the best bets to enter? Are there any optimum entries? *The National Lottery Magazine's* team of EXPERTS will guide your hand.

Subscribe now and GAIN AN ADVANTAGE. That million may be just around the corner!

A full year's subscription is normally £59.50. But as a special once-only introductory offer for purchasers of *The National lottery Book*, you can receive *The National Lottery Magazine* for a year for **ONLY £19.95**.

A small price to pay for

The chance to change your life!
Order form on the last page.

More details can be obtained by writing to The National Lottery Magazine, The Lottery Company, PO Box 200, Harrogate HG1 4XB.

- ❑ Mouse driven.
- ❑ Pop-down menus.
- ❑ Multiple resizeable windows.
- ❑ Save, view, print any window.
- ❑ Modify screen colours.
- ❑ Over seven years development.

Autocorrelation - Trend analysis.

This particularly powerful part of the programme can *find patterns that the human mind cannot detect*, in a matter of seconds. The algorithms are transparent to the user and will help you pick winning patterns from previous lottery draws and pools results. These techniques are used extensively by the scientific and engineering worlds in processes that require pattern identification and recognition, e.g. robot machine vision, radio astronomy (finding new stars, solar systems and galaxies!), and radar signature analysis.

By covering more numbers you can win more often. Lotto Factory includes a massive 254 pre-defined GUARANTEED systems that allow you to cover more numbers at a lower cost than conventional systems.

EXAMPLE

If you are playing a Lotto Factory '5 from 6' wheeling system with 12 numbers and on the night of the draw 6 of your 12 numbers come home - then you are GUARANTEED AT LEAST ONE SECOND PRIZE worth many thousands of pounds!

Lotto Factory
- By Far Superior!

How LOTTO FACTORY works:

(1) First pick your winning numbers, up to 45 can be chosen.
  (a) Autocorrelation trend analysis.
  (b) Highest winning system scan.
  (c) Statistical Analysis.

(2) Then choose games using computer intelligence to include as many numbers as possible while incurring minimal cost.
  (a) Pre-defined systems or game plans.
  (b) User-defined systems or game plans.

(3) Save some money by reducing the number of games that have to be played in your generated system.
  (a) Delete redundant games.

(4) Next use some advanced statistics to save even more money on your system entry.
  (a) Delete Bell-Curve redundant games.
  (b) Define your own % winning chance.

(5) Odds/Evens reduction.

(6) Test your wheeling system and ensure your number selection method has worked in the past.

(7) Update previous draw data file.

As you can see, Lotto Factory is NOT just a programme that generates random numbers and checks your winnings. It is only for those who are serious about wanting to win significant cash prizes in the lottery.

Given the **POTENTIAL REWARDS** of even a minor win in the lottery the cost of Lotto Factory is minimal. For only £89.50 including packing and postage, you will receive the most advanced lottery software available. **Even the smallest of wins will re-coup the purchase cost many times over. And by saving money on each entry, you should soon be in profit. YOUR million could be just a keystroke away**

Order form on last page

Order form on last page

System requirements: IBM PC, AT, XT compatible, 640K RAM, 3½" 720K/1.44M or 5¼" 360K/1.2M floppy disk drive, CGA/EGA/ VGA compatible monitor and card, MS-DOS.

GIFT BOOKS

Saving Money Made Simple
Find out how to cut the costs of running your car... decorating your home... repaying your mortgage... valuable tips which could save you up to £100,000. £2.99

Making Money Made Simple
Ever dreamed of becoming wealthy? Then this is the book for you. Packed with tips and inspiration from people who have made it to the top of the money tree. £3.99

Rude Cats (for cat lovers everywhere)
If you have ever wondered what your average moggie has been up to as it staggers back over the garden wall, covered in scar tissue and licking its rear end, then "RUDE CATS" is for you. Join Randy, an old campaigner on a sexually explicit journey of discovery into the twilight world beyond the cat-flap and prepare to be shocked! £3.99

The Armchair Guide to Football
An inexpensive and humorous look at the state of modern football. Is it really run by money crazed businessmen who don't care about tradition? Will Fantasy Football remove the need for pitches, players and footballs? Only £1.99

The Armchair Guide to Fishing
Just why do people go fishing? Is it the basic hunting instinct or do they just love drowning maggots? Only £1.99

The Armchair Guide to Golf
From the serious handicap hunter to the weekend hacker, everybody involved with golf will appreciate this humorous view from the 'inside'. Only £1.99

A Load of Bollards
Road cones. Breeding like rabbits. Moving only at night. Causing chaos as they appear from nowhere. Will the motorists nightmare never end? £3.99

Sex Trivia: The Bedside Guide
Does sex turn you on? Then here's a bedside companion that's titillating, weird, erotic, bizarre, sizzling, shocking, hilarious... and packed with thousands of TRUE FACTS! £3.99

Down the Pan: Amuse Yourself in the Toilet
Here is an hilarious collection of cartoons, jokes and silly stories... great toilet accidents... secret bog card tricks... famous toilets of history... even learn how to juggle toilet rolls! £3.99

For a free full colour catalogue of all titles, please send an SAE to the address below.

Order form on last page

HUMOUR BOOKS

The Ancient Art of Farting by Dr. C.Huff
Ever since time began, man (not woman) has farted. Does this ability lie behind many of the so far unexplained mysteries of history? You Bet - because Dr. C.Huff's research shows conclusively there's something rotten about history taught in schools. If you do most of your reading on the throne, then this book is your ideal companion. Sit back and fart yourself silly as you split your sides laughing! *£3.99*

A Wunch of Bankers
Do you HATE BANKS? Then you need this collection of stories aimed directly at the crotch of your bank manager. A Wunch of Bankers mixes cartoons and jokes about banks with real-life horror stories of the bare-faced money-grabbing tactics of banks. If you think you've been treated badly, read these stories!!!! *£3.99*

The Hangover Handbook & Boozer's Bible
(In the shape of a beercan)
Ever groaned, burped and cursed the morning after, as Vesuvius erupted in your stomach, a bass drummer thumped on your brain and a canary fouled its nest in your throat? Then you need these 100+ hangover remedies. There's an exclusive Hangover Ratings Chart, a Boozer's Calendar, a Hangover Clinic, and you can meet the Great Drunks of History, try the Boozer's Reading Chart, etc., etc. *£3.99*

The Beerlover's Bible & Homebar Handbook
(also in the shape of a beercan)
Do you love beer? Then this is the book you've been waiting for - a tantalising brew of fascinating facts to help you enjoy your favourite fluid all the more. Discover how to serve beer for maximum enjoyment... brew your own... entertain with beer... cook tasty recipes... and more! Includes an exhaustive listing of beers from all over the world with their flavours, colours and potency. You'll become a walking encyclopedia on beer! £3.99

A Slow Screw Against the wall (& Other Cocktails)
Over 200 recipes for luscious and lively cocktails. Even the most serious of cocktail drinkers will find something new for their taste buds to savour. £3.99

The Bog Book
(In the shape of a toilet seat)
How much time do you spend in the bog every day? Are you letting valuable time go to waste? Not any longer! Now you can spend every second to your advantage. The Bog Book is packed with enough of the funny, the weird and the wonderful to drive you potty. Fill your brain while you empty your bowels! *£3.99*

Order form on last page

EXPRESS ORDER FORM

If you would rather not damage your copy of *The National Lottery Book*, please use plain paper and remember to include all the details listed below!

Postage for books is FREE within the U.K.
Please add £1 per title in other EEC countries and £3 elsewhere.

Order by phone or fax with your credit card details on

01423-507545

Quantity		Value
....	The National Lottery Magazine £19.95	....
	(1 year subscription at discounted price for book purchasors only)	
....	Lotto Factory £79.50	....
....	LottoMAGIC *(shareware copying and distribution)* £12.95	....
....	Making Money Made Simple £3.99	....
....	Saving Money Made Simple ~~£3.99~~ £2.99	....
....	Sex Trivia: The Bedside Guide £3.99	....
....	Down the Pan: Amuse Yourself in the Toilet £3.99	....
....	The Ancient Art of Farting £3.99	....
....	A Wunch of Bankers £3.99	....
....	The Hangover Handbook & Boozer's Bible £3.99	....
....	The Beerlover's Bible & Homebar Handbook £3.99	....
....	A Slow Screw Against the Wall £3.99	....
....	The Bog Book £3.99	....
....	Rude Cats £3.99	....
....	The Armchair Guide to Football £1.99	....
....	The Armchair Guide to Fishing £1.99	....
....	The Armchair Guide to Golf £1.99	....

TOTAL _____

I enclose a cheque/Postal Order for £ _____
made payable to 'Take That Ltd.'

Please debit my ☐ Access ☐ Visa

Card number: ☐☐☐☐ ☐☐☐☐ ☐☐☐☐ ☐☐☐☐ ☐☐☐☐

Expiry date: ☐☐☐☐

Signature: Date:

Name: _____

Address: _____

_____ Postcode: _____

Please return to: Take That Books, P.O.Box 200, Harrogate, HG1 4XB

Please allow 14-21 days delivery. We hope to make you further exciting offers in the future. If you do not wish to receive these, please write to us at the above address.   natlotbk